DOLLARS & UNCOMMON SENSE

BASIC TRAINING FOR YOUR MONEY

STEVE REPAK, CFP®

Published by
RFS Publishing
Savannah, Georgia 31406

ISBN: 978-0-9839011-0-5

First Printing

Printed in the United States of America

Cover and Interior Design by GKS Creative

Library of Congress information on file with the Publisher

DOLLARS &
UNCOMMON
SENSE

BASIC TRAINING
FOR YOUR MONEY

God, family, country, and friends, thank you!

I praise God for His many blessings.

I dedicate this book to my family, as without their love and support, I would not have had the strength to complete it.

To the members of our armed services and their families, thank you so much for the many sacrifices you make each and every day so we can live freely and prosper in this great nation.

Contents

Foreword

I first met my friend Steve Repak while speaking at a series of Financial Readiness Challenge events run by the Department of Defense to help military personnel and their families manage their finances effectively. As the author of *Privacy Means Profit* and several other books on identity theft, social media exposure, and weapons of manipulation, my task was to motivate our service members during a keynote speech to care about one very important aspect of financial health: identity theft protection. Steve, meanwhile, spoke to groups and gave one-on-one counseling on other vital aspects of financial health: saving, spending, and taking control of debt.

What impressed me about Steve was that he always gave practical advice that anyone could follow, and he empowered his audience to take charge of their own finances. One thing that really stood out for me was the way he got his point across—by making his audience laugh, by talking straight, and by telling his own personal story of digging his way out of debt. Many years ago, he was struggling like so many people are; but he became his own boss and a very successful and trusted financial planner. Having been there in the financial trenches gives him the credibility to truly inspire people to change their lives. During his presentations, you could see the wheels start to turn in their minds. It was great to see people who were worried about their finances but didn't know where to begin finally get the advice and the push they needed.

I could tell that Steve spoke from experience, about what he has seen work for his clients in his own financial planning business and what has worked for him. In *Dollars & Uncommon Sense*, he has drawn together in one book all the wisdom and experience about reducing debt, controlling spending, and building up savings. When I read it, I could hear Steve's voice, like back at those Financial Readiness Challenge events. He gets his message across with his usual warmth, humor, and straight talk. What he delivers should be common sense, but unfortunately it's not—until you've read his book. *Dollars & Uncommon Sense* is for anyone who wants to finally take control of their finances, get out of debt once and for all, be prepared for financial emergencies and the next economic downturn, and live the life they want in retirement.

With Steve to guide the way, I wish you all the best in your own personal quest for a secure financial future.

John Sileo

John Sileo is the founder of ThinkLikeASpy.com, the award-winning author of *Privacy Means Profit*, and America's leading professional speaker on identity theft, social media exposure, and data breach.

Introduction

Most people fight about one of three things: money, sex, and kids. I am not going to give you any advice on how to raise your kids, and most likely you don't want my sex advice, but I can change the way you think about money. I can empower you to be free from debt, take control of your finances, and have more money.

In my 12 years as a financial planner, by observing my clients, I have learned why some people are so good at building wealth while most people have sleepless nights worrying about their financial future. By learning to think and behave the same way as the wealth builders who came through my door (and avoiding the mistakes the others made), I was able to build my own successful business as a financial planner and to build my family's wealth. What I learned I am now sharing with you in *Dollars & Uncommon Sense*.

But the journey that led me to writing this book actually began long before that, when I was just 18 years old, stepping off the bus in Fort Dix, New Jersey, with a drill sergeant yelling at me to line up in formation. I knew that basic training wasn't supposed to be a picnic, but I had no idea I would have this 6 foot 2 inch monster in my face screaming obscenities at me. Once everybody got off the bus and lined up, the drill sergeant came up to me and asked why I was eyeballing him. I had no idea what he was talking about, but I thought that maybe if I curled up in a ball on the ground, he might quit hollering. I did not curl up in a ball, and he did not quit hollering.

The transition from civilian life to military life was not going to be easy. Change is never easy, so if anyone tells you any differently, they are lying. The first step in my transformation was to start looking like a soldier. I grew up in the '80s, so I had the "hair." At the time, it was called a tri-level haircut, but using current terminology, it would be called the "Sean Cassidy Mullet." I had some really nice hair, but in less than a blink of an eye, it was gone and I looked like a Q-tip, as did the rest of the guys around me.

After the haircut, we were marched to get a physical and then shots. Once everyone had been stuck and prodded, we were then marched to a warehouse to get our gear. I remember trying on my BDU, or battle dress uniform. That was the first moment I started realizing that my identity and old life as a civilian were gone. I wasn't a fully fledged soldier yet, but I looked the part. That night, everyone took shifts on fire guard. Fire guard is where you walk through the barracks to make sure that no fires had broken out. At the time, I did not understand why I had to walk around at night making sure that the concrete building didn't catch on fire, but now I know that it was part of the process by which I was slowly being transformed in order to change the way I thought. I had no choice in the matter if I was going to survive the next eight grueling weeks.

In basic training, a soldier goes through a process of mental and emotional retraining so that he can operate in an environment very different from the civilian world. He also learns fundamental skills so that he will be ready for anything. *Dollars & Uncommon Sense* is the money equivalent: I will guide you through a process of mental and emotional retraining that will *transform the way you think about money* and give you the *fundamental skills* you need to build wealth. The aim is that you will begin to think differently and do different things with your money—and as a result, you will be able to grow your wealth in ways that most people simply never do.

Although basic training in the military was not one of my most enjoyable experiences, it did shape my life in a positive way and helped me become the person I am today. Likewise, retraining the way you think about money won't be easy at first. I am not some drill sergeant who's going to scream obscenities at you, but I am also not going to sugarcoat things for you. I'll tell it like it really is. This means that sometime in this process, you will probably have to face painful truths about your relationship with money. You will need to go through a period of adjustment, like the one I went through after I got off the bus in Fort Dix. But it will be worth it, because just as basic training made me who I am today, you will be positively transformed by this process.

In this book, I don't offer you a magic formula or new technique for having more money—because there isn't one. The basic principles for building wealth have been available to you for years. The key to being able to use them effectively is changing the way you think about money. From now on, you will no longer use common sense when making financial decisions but start using *uncommon* sense. Uncommon sense is when you think and do things differently from most people. As soon as you start thinking differently, you will begin *doing* things differently with your money.

In Part 1, we're going to take a look at the new thinking habits you will need in order to become a successful wealth builder. I'll also share with you the 6 Key Traits of Wealth Builders that I have learned by observing how the wealthy think about money.

In Part 2, you will learn to take control of your spending. This is the fundamental first step, because you could have the biggest salary in the world, but if you don't know where your money's going and you don't have a spending plan, you're still going to be broke.

Most people find it hard to even think about planning for their future because right now they're saddled with credit card debt. In Part 3, you will learn why debt is so damaging, and we'll go step-by-step through the process of becoming debt free once and for all.

In Part 4, we will talk about how to get your money working for you by saving and investing it. Most people are overwhelmed by all the jargon of investing. By the end of this book, you will not be most people.

Most people were also not prepared for one of the hardest-hitting recessions since the Great Depression. I cannot predict the future, but history often repeats itself. So I am going to prepare you for the next financial crisis when it does happen. You will be ready, the same way a soldier who has been through basic training is ready for anything.

My intention is for the advice in this book to be taken literally. *Dollars & Uncommon Sense* is not intended as a series of ideas for you to think about but as a practical, step-by-step program for retraining the way you think about and act with money. Basic training is highly effective in part because it retrains recruits to follow instructions as a reflex. Similarly, the more closely you stick to this program, the more successful your transformation will be. Better financial thinking and behavior will become a reflex.

"Change the way you think" is not just some cute catchphrase I've used to get you to purchase the book. It is what you *need* to do in order to be prepared for the next financial battle. Open your mind and take the steps I outline, and you will have the tools and the outlook you need to transform your finances and your life.

Part 1
Basic Training

1: Change the Way You Think

Most people scratch their heads and wonder why they are in the same financial predicament as everybody else. Assess the situation around you. Look at your friends, family, and neighbors. How many people do you know who live paycheck to paycheck? Do you know anyone who is worried about how they're going to pay their rent or mortgage, or what they're going to do about grocery money? Do you know someone whose utilities are on the verge of being cut off? Can you think of anyone you know who is worrying about how they'll get by if they lose their job? Are you one of them?

Perhaps, like most people, you are stressing over how much debt you have and are just making minimum payments on all of your credit cards. Are you looking for a way out? Or are you coping with the problem by telling yourself that everybody you know is in debt, so it must be okay that you are, too?

Retirement? What's that? Are you thinking you will be dead by then, so you don't have to worry about that now?

I could go on forever and ever. The truth is that most people are living paycheck to paycheck.[1] Most people have some sort of debt they are worried about. Most people worry about losing their job and wonder how they will pay their bills if that happens. Most people wait until they are 55 to even start thinking about retirement. Most people worry about their money.

> *Most people worry about their money. So why in the heck would you want to be like most people?*

So why in the heck would you want to be like most people?

These days I am happy to say that I am not like most people. But to tell you the truth, I used to be.

When I was growing up, my family had little or no money. I lived in a trailer park. Both of my parents worked hard, and I never went hungry and always had a shelter over my head. I had clothes to wear, but at times, kids made fun of what I was wearing. Neither of my parents went to college, so education wasn't stressed that much. As long as I had passing grades, they were happy. As I got older, I took part-time jobs after school for extra money. After graduating high school, I enlisted in the Army.

I was just like everybody else with my money. I spent everything I made, lived paycheck to paycheck, and had no savings to speak of. I really didn't understand why I needed savings. I only had a little debt, I thought. But the truth was that I racked up more than $32,000 in credit card debt. I thought that was okay. I told

---

1   In a 2010 study, 77 percent of American workers reported that they were living paycheck to paycheck. Study conducted by Harris Interactive© on behalf of CareerBuilder.com among 2,534 U.S. hiring managers and 4,498 U.S. workers, May–June 2010.

myself that everybody has credit card debt and that it couldn't be a problem, because I was able to make the minimum payments each month. As for retirement, I was young and thought to myself that I would worry about that later.

I worked my way up the ranks, and after 12 years of service I decided to move on. From the contacts I made in the military, I was offered a job in finance. I hadn't set out to make a career in finance, but someone saw a talent in me that I hadn't recognized yet myself. And it was the best thing that could have ever happened to me. What I am going to tell you next is what started me on the path to changing the way I think about money.

I spent everything I made, lived paycheck to paycheck, and had no savings to speak of.

It was the first time I saw real money. I was an investment representative for a national broker-dealer in El Paso, Texas, and I had been in the business for only a few weeks. A couple in their 40s came into my office and told my receptionist that they needed help investing some of their savings. She showed them into my office, they sat down, and I started gathering information from them. They were just normal-looking people. They didn't look or act rich, I thought to myself. I told them that before I could open an account, I had to find out where the money was coming from— for example, insurance proceeds, the selling of a business, or an inheritance. The couple told me the money was part of what they had in their savings. After I completed the paperwork, they wrote a personal check for $25,000 to be deposited into their account. I still remember to this day how my hands were shaking when they placed that check into them. I never knew that normal people could have that kind of money. I didn't know that ordinary people could write a personal check for that much! I thought only people with rich parents or an inheritance had money and that the only way regular people could ever have money like that was if they won the lottery or something.

I wasn't totally convinced yet that regular people could have money in their savings accounts without luck, but this was the day my mind-set started to shift.

I want to share another story with you that also happened very early in my career and confirmed that I really *did* need to start thinking differently about money. On this day, I had two appointments scheduled, one in the morning and the other in the afternoon. Looking out the window, I saw my first client, a lady in her early 50s, drive up in a nice European sports car. As my receptionist escorted her into my office, I thought to myself that she was wearing a pretty expensive-looking wardrobe.

The first thing she told me was that she was an executive who worked for a software company. She went on to tell me that her salary was close to $300,000 a year. In the back of my head, the wheels were turning. I was thinking, "She must have a ton of money she wants invested." Then she told me that she had to exercise some of her company stock options because she was about $50,000 in debt with her credit cards and could no longer make the minimum payments.

I wondered to myself how anyone who made that much money could have problems making the minimum payments on her credit cards. I know the answer now, but at that time, I was still thinking like most people.

That afternoon, my second appointment arrived. I saw her drive up in her late-model sedan. She was nicely dressed but wearing nothing as fancy as my first appointment had worn. I asked her to tell me a little bit about herself. She told me she was a schoolteacher, her salary was about $30,000 a year, and she was about to retire.

I am embarrassed to admit that I remember thinking to myself that she probably didn't have a lot of money to invest. When I asked her how much she wanted me to manage, I almost fell out of my chair: She had close to $400,000 in her retirement account.

I thought to myself, "How in the heck could a schoolteacher who doesn't earn much accumulate so much wealth?"

Scenarios like this have played out time and again in my office over the years. The most important lesson I have learned from this is: It doesn't matter how much education you have or how much money you make, it's *the way you think about money* that determines how much money you have. The reason most people are bad with money is that they believe they are bad with it. They believe they can't do anything about it. They believe they will never have more of it. Your first step is to quit thinking this way.

> *It doesn't matter how much education you have or how much money you make, it's **the way you think about money** that determines how much you have.*

Most of my clients are 55 or older. On average, they have between $500,000 and $1 million of investable assets. (I usually don't like working with people with more than a million, because they think they are smarter than me . . . which may be true!) What I want you to take away is not *how much* money my clients have, but *how they got* their money. Most of my clients are just average people. Most of them were not corporate executives, doctors, or lawyers. Over the years of managing my clients' wealth, I have found that they share common traits in how they think about money and, as a consequence, what they do with it. I call these the 6 Key Traits of Wealth Builders:

1. They spend less money than they make.
2. They have little or no debt.
3. They save.
4. They have long-term plans for their money.
5. They do not let emotions cloud their judgment when they make financial decisions.
6. They start saving early in their careers.

You might not have any control over that last one if you've already been in the workforce for a while and are only now getting serious about your money. That's okay, because if you take a look at the other five key traits, you *do* have control over those.

This works for everyone, not just clients of financial planners. I know this because a few years ago, in addition to managing people's wealth, I started doing consulting work as a contractor for the Department of Defense. On the weekends, I speak to service members and their families and provide them with free financial education and counseling. I really love doing that, because I know that if someone had taught me to think differently about money back when I was in the Army, I would have been so much better off.

Well, over the past few years I've discovered that the 6 Key Traits of Wealth Builders apply to people in the service, too. Since I have been in the military, I know that you really don't make that much money. Yet when I met with these people, I learned that some of them had been able to accumulate a good sum of money. I asked them about their backgrounds, and it turned out their wealth had nothing to do with their rank or education level. The servicemen and women with money were those who spent less than they made, took on little or no debt, saved, planned for the long term, kept emotions out of their financial decisions, and started early.

The bottom line is that *you don't have to make a lot of money to have a lot of money*. If you learn to spend less, you will have more. It sounds

You don't have to make a lot of money to have a lot of money.

so easy, and it is something you probably already know. The difference is that in the following chapters we are now going to do something about it, by changing the way you think about money— and then you will begin to change what you *do* with your money.

THE TAKE HOME

- Most people worry about their money. You don't want to be like most people.
- It doesn't matter how much education you have or how much money you make, it's *the way you think about money* that determines how much money you have.
- There are 6 Key Traits of Wealth Builders:

1. They spend less money than they make.
2. They have little or no debt.
3. They save.
4. They have long-term plans for their money.
5. They do not let emotions cloud their judgment when they make financial decisions.
6. They start saving early in their careers.

- You don't have to make a lot of money to have a lot of money. If you learn to spend less, you will have more.

2: Build Your Foundations

If you don't change the way you think about money, there is no way you will change the things you do with your money. To achieve your financial goals, or in fact any goal, you need to start out with a strong foundation. Without a strong foundation, you will fall back into the same routine you have been in for years. In order for you to start thinking differently, you will need to change the three Ps: your *principles*, *priorities*, and *plans*. When you change all three, you will establish the foundation for how you will make decisions about your finances. You will finally be able to reach your personal money goals.

Without a strong foundation, you will fall back into the same routine you have been in for years.

Let's begin with *principles*.

PRINCIPLES

A *principle* is a basic truth that serves as the foundation for how you live your life. It is a core belief. In Chapter 1, we talked about a number of principles that people hold about money. One person might believe that only people who are born wealthy or win the lottery will ever have money and that it doesn't matter what ordinary people do, they will never have money. Another might believe that if people spend less than they earn, always put a little away in savings, and make financial decisions with their heads rather than their hearts, they will grow their wealth. Naturally, these different principles will lead these two people to do very different things with their money.

PRIORITIES

Every day we set priorities for ourselves, basing them on what we think is most important or urgent for us to do, or what our main concern is. But when we're busy, we can get so caught up responding to what needs to be done *right now* that we lose focus on the big picture. Here is a simple question to ask yourself: What am I spending my time on, and what am I spending my money on? If you give yourself a moment to think about this, you might be surprised to find that what you are actually prioritizing might not be what you *should* be prioritizing.

Most people do not make their finances a priority. That is a big mistake. Think of a time when you had to reset your priorities at work or at home because something urgent came up. As soon as you changed your priorities, you started thinking differently and doing different things. For this reason, in this book we are going to take a close look at your money priorities.

No one else is going to start managing your money better for you. You need to reset your own priorities, and then things will start changing for you. The fact that you have purchased this book shows that you already have some of your priorities in order. You have spent money on something that is important. You have acknowledged to yourself that you want your finances to be different, and you put your money where your mouth is.

> *No one else is going to start managing your money better for you.*

PLANS

I have heard over and over again that people do not plan to fail. I don't believe that. Most people fail because they don't have a plan, so the real truth is that they are planning to fail, they just haven't written it down yet! Because you do not want to be like most people, you are going to change that, starting today.

Most people have good intentions and know it would be a smart idea if they wrote down a plan for their money. So why don't they? They equate planning with changing, and you know as well as I do that most peo-

> *Most people fail because they don't have a plan.*

ple do not like change. The tragedy here is that by avoiding the short-term pain of adapting to change, these people are missing out on long-term positive change in their finances. Most of these people in fact are at risk of a retirement in which they may not be able to pay their heating bill or buy groceries. To build wealth, you need to change your attitude and actions with money, and that means acknowledging to yourself that you need to plan.

Planning involves long-term thinking, and if you want more

money, you have to start thinking longer term. In the chapters that follow, we will go step-by-step through setting up plans for your spending, debt repayment, saving, and investing. In each instance, you will assess where you are now, then you'll develop the right plan for you, and finally you'll put it into practice. From time to time, you will review and adjust the plan so that it's still leading you toward your ultimate goal.

A final word on plans: They need to be written down. If you write a plan down, you have a much higher probability of following it.

HOW THE THREE P'S WORK TOGETHER

The person who believes that it is only those who are born wealthy or win the lottery who will ever have money probably follows few or no rules about how to spend money, doesn't give money a high priority, and does little or no planning. On the other hand, the person who believes people can change their financial destiny probably follows a number of money rules, gives money a high priority, and has a long-term financial plan. (I think you know by now which of these people ends up with the most money.) It is important to remember that while changing your principles is the crucial first step, you will then need to follow it through by actually *doing* something different with your money. Your priorities and plans will be the new framework for what you *do* with your money.

As an example, let's consider this principle: "If you identify and reduce your wasteful spending, you will have more money." The first stage is to embrace this *principle* and admit that you are wasting money. Then you will need to set new *priorities*; your first will be to spend on what you need rather than what you want.

Finally, you will make a new spending *plan* to ensure that you cut your wasteful spending by 15 percent. If you believe that you are wasting money, you will reduce the amount you are spending. If you then follow the plan of cutting your wasteful spending by 15 percent, you will have more money.

> *Most people say they want to be better with their money, but they don't do anything differently.*

What I have just shared with you isn't anything miraculous, but the truth is that most people say they want to be better with their money, but they don't do anything differently. It's important to balance thinking and doing, so in the following chapters, we are going to look in turn at the principles, priorities, and plans you need to follow in order to become a wealth builder.

Your First Principle

People who write down their goals have a higher probability of reaching them.

In fact, a prominent psychologist has stated that it is possible that people are 11 times more likely to reach a goal when they write it down, as opposed to simply thinking about the goal.[2]

I believe that the physical act of writing transforms a thought into an action. Keep this in mind: Most people do not write down their goals. Most people fail to reach their goals. You do not want to be like most people, so from now on, write your financial goals down.

---

2   Jack N. Singer, Ph.D., says you are 11 times more likely to reach a goal if you write it down. See www.calgaryschild.com/workplace/832-surefire-strategies-for-success-over-stress-how-to-build-lasting-resilience, accessed on May 26, 2011.

Throughout this program, you will be setting goals and using worksheets to assess and plan your spending and saving, so now is the time to set up a system for keeping all of that material on record. Some people like to buy a blank journal to write in; others like to file their money goals and plans in a folder. The key is to find a system that suits you and enables you to keep everything in one place, where you can easily access it.

Your First Priority

Make finances a top priority.

Did you know that most people watch an average of 35 hours of television a week?[3] I want you to spend at least one hour of your time each week on your money. Choose the same day and time each week, block out that hour in your diary or on your calendar, and then show up like you would for any appointment. Your money has to be one of your top priorities, so don't allow anything else to take your attention at that time.

Your First Plan

Read this book right through to the end.

The sad truth is that most people read only the first few pages of a nonfiction book. *Dollars & Uncommon Sense* is basic training for your finances, and it is designed as a program to be followed from beginning to end. Only by approaching it that way will you be able to completely transform the way you think about money. That's why I've kept it short, clear, and easy to follow: I want you to read it from cover to cover in one sitting, so that

---

3   People in the United States with TVs spend on average 158 hours, 25 minutes each month tuning in to television, according to Nielsen's Three Screen Report for the first quarter of 2010.

you get the big picture. The book is designed to be read in just a few hours.

If you have the time right now to keep on reading, that's great. Otherwise, pick a good time—one night during the week or one weekend—when you can make it a priority to read and absorb this book. Write that day down in your diary or calendar as you would any appointment, and show up on time. This is about your financial future, so treat it as though it's a doctor's appointment that you have been trying to schedule for the past six months and you know there won't be any other openings anytime soon.

Because *Dollars & Uncommon Sense* is all about retraining the way you think about and act with money, the changes I'm recommending won't happen overnight. This is a step-by-step process that will change the way you spend, pay off debt, save, and invest. When you complete one step, you will need to open the book again and take a look at the next step, so that you remember what you need to do. This is the kind of book that I hope you will use your highlighter on, so that later on you can find key ideas again when you need to refresh your memory or renew your commitment to the principles.

As in basic training in the military, repetitiveness is a key to building competence and confidence. When you read things over and over again, they start to become second nature and you are able to start thinking differently without any effort. Once you start thinking differently, goals you thought you could never reach start seeming reachable, because you have the tools and competence you need to succeed. And as each of your goals are met, you build more confidence.

Congratulations, you have just completed your initial orientation! In the next chapter, you will learn how to start taking charge of your money. You will start telling it where to go, instead of having no idea where it went.

THE TAKE HOME

- To start thinking differently, you will need to change the three Ps: your *principles*, *priorities*, and *plans*.
- Principles are core beliefs that influence what you do with your money.
- Priorities are what you spend your time and money on. As soon as you change your priorities, you start thinking differently and doing different things with your money.
- Write down your long-term financial plans and goals, and review and adjust them regularly.
- Spend at least one hour of your time each week on your money.
- Set aside a time to read this book through, then review it again each time you complete one of the steps.

Part 2
Spending

3: Principle: If You Spend Less, You Will Have More

I assume that the primary reason you purchased this book is because you want more money. Most people think that the only way they will ever have more money is if they either win the lottery or receive it from an inheritance. First, if you think you are going to win the lottery, the chances of winning are low. Take Powerball in North Carolina, where I live: Your chance of hitting the jackpot is 1 in 195 million.[4] Not good odds.

Even if you do win the lottery, haven't you watched any of those television specials showing that most lottery winners end up going bankrupt? If you are one of the rare lucky ones who does win the lottery, you will most likely still end up in the same predicament you are in today, wondering why you have little or no money.

As for the inheritance plan, if you have a rich relative, you most likely wouldn't have purchased this book, but I am going to reveal

---

4   North Carolina Education Lottery Policies and Procedures, Chapter 8—Sales, September 7, 2010, www.nc-educationlottery.org/uploads/docs/8.04A%20Powerball%20Game%20Rules.pdf, accessed May 26, 2011.

a secret to you anyway: *You will not have more money just because you have more money.*

I know you are probably scratching your head and thinking this is crazy talk. How can having more money *not* result in having more money?

The answer is that unless you change the way you spend, you will never have more money. If you did win a $1 million lottery prize, but afterward you spent $1.5 million, you would be worse off than before you won. A more common example is when people think that their next raise will finally get them out of their financial dilemma, yet they just get further into debt. Similarly, most people who know they are going to receive a tax refund, a year-end bonus check, or some other windfall, have that money spent way before they even get it. You are no different. You are normal. You are wired that way.

> *Unless you change the way you spend, you will never have more money.*

WIRED TO SPEND

Have you ever read a book or taken a class to learn about saving money? There's a good chance you have. I have a more telling question, though: Have you ever read a book or taken a class to learn how to *spend* your money? You are probably laughing out loud and thinking, "I don't need a class on that. Spending money is easy; nobody has to teach me how to spend!" That is where most people get it wrong.

The reason most people don't have money has nothing to do with how much they make or have. The problem has to do with *spending*. We can all use some training in how to spend properly.

If you're like most people, you love spending money. Spending money makes you feel good! Your feelings control how, when, and where you choose to spend your precious dollars. This is not a secret, and many companies take advantage of it. They know that consumers are swayed heavily by their emotions in their purchasing decisions. Television commercials can get you to buy things that you might not really need, because the pleasure-seeking part of the brain, rather than the logical part, makes the decision.

We are vulnerable to all kinds of signals that influence our emotions and our behavior. For instance, the color red signifies danger, and black signifies death. Notice that those are the colors the news channels use to sensationalize breaking news. This gets your attention and keeps you glued to the TV, and in turn the news channels make money from advertisers trying to sell you things. Remember, without an audience, there is nobody for them to sell their stuff to. It is not a conspiracy, but companies are in the business to make money. How do they do this? By taking *your* money. Or more accurately, by getting you to *give* them your money.

From a very early age, you are exposed to a world that wants your money. Everybody wants it. (Including me!) You are bombarded with television commercials, sales in the newspaper, ads on the internet, and in the meantime, some *Everybody wants your money.* marketing person is trying to come up with another creative way to separate you from your money.

We live in a culture of spending. We live in a culture of immediate gratification. We live in a culture that looks favorably on being in debt. And it feels so good to spend, spend, spend! Perhaps you buy a video game. You play and play and play that video game until you beat the game. It makes you feel good. After that, you go to the store and buy another video game, play it until you beat it, then go back to the store . . . and the madness goes on forever. Or maybe to feel good you go and buy new shoes or the latest designer jeans you saw a celebrity wear in your favorite magazine. The high doesn't last long, they go out of fashion, and pretty soon you're back at the store doing it all over again. Whatever it is you like to buy, you're spending money because it makes you feel good in the short term. Let's not forget, people who have money think *long term*.

So why do most people think short term? A phenomenon termed *availability bias* causes us to base our decisions on our most recent and meaningful experiences. That is, *how we feel at the moment* influences the way we make decisions.

Here is a familiar example that shows how availability bias works. I have been going to the same gym for years now, and in January, I always joke with my friends about the "New Year's resolutioners." Their reasons for wanting to get into better shape are many. Some want to get ready for an upcoming reunion or other event, and some just want to look good in their swimsuit by summer. They start out on the right path but find out after a week or so that if they want to be fit, they are going to have to eat right and exercise. One by one, they stop coming to the gym.

Regardless of their goals, the most common cause for their failure is availability bias. Short-term feelings interfere with beneficial long-term results. In other words, they let the soreness in their muscles or the fact that it would be much more fun to eat pizza in front of the TV cause them to quit. They are unsuccessful with the goal of getting into shape. Don't let this happen to you when it comes to your goal of getting into better financial shape. Rather than giving in to short-term emotions (the high you get from buying something), think about your long-term goal (a financially secure future).

WHY MAKING MORE MONEY ISN'T THE ANSWER

It is a misconception that making more money will help you have more money. I liken it to the relationship between eating and exercise: You can exercise all day long, but if you are eating more calories than you are burning off, you will never lose weight.

In the military, the way you make more money is by being promoted, and promotions are based on how much time in grade—that is, time in a particular rank—and how much time in service you have overall. For example, most people when they enlist in the Army begin at the lowest rank, which is Private E-1. Unless you get into some type of trouble, after being in for six months, you will be promoted to Private E-2. After you have 18 months of service and at least four months as an E-2, you will be promoted to Private First Class E-3.

As long as I didn't get in trouble and could pass my physical fitness test and meet a few other prerequisites, I had a pretty good idea of when I would be promoted and start to make more money. When I was making $1,500 a month, and I knew that in three months I would be making $1,800, I would spend that much. I did this every promotion, from when I was an E-1 through to an E-7. And as you know, I ended up seriously in debt.

From all the people in the Army who I have counseled and spoken to, I have discovered that I wasn't the only one who thought that way. Time and time again, people who are having problems making ends meet tell me that the problem is going to get fixed when they are promoted next month, or when they take this special assignment, or when they get their tax refund check, or when they get their reenlistment bonus. Get the idea? Most people believe that they will be in a better financial situation as soon as they make more money, yet when they do begin making more money, they just start spending more money.

Whether you make $100 a week or $100,000 a week, if you spend more than what you make, you will be broke.

You might be thinking to yourself that this applies only to people who are on low incomes. In fact, I have clients who are making anywhere between $70,000 and $350,000 a year in salary and can't make ends meet. My best friend, Derrell, who manages wealth in Birmingham, Alabama, had to put two of his clients on a strict budget because they were spending more than $8,000 a month just on clothes! This couple was making more than $500,000 a year and would need grocery money. The point is: Whether you make $100 a week or $100,000 a week, if you spend more than you make, you will be broke.

So when I say "Have you ever taken a class on spending?" I am really not joking around. I can't stress enough this principle: *If you spend less, you will have more.*

ADMIT YOU HAVE A PROBLEM

You need to be more careful when you are spending your money. Did you notice I didn't say *smarter*? Even smart people spend their money on stupid stuff.

I tell people that there are only a few things that you really need. They are food, shelter, transportation, clothing, and companionship—and you shouldn't be paying for that last one. The problem is that most people confuse the things they *want* with the things they *need*. For example, you need food, but do you need to go out to a restaurant three times a week? You need transportation, but do you need the new Escalade? Most people like that new-car smell, but after your stinky butt has been sitting in the car for a few months, the new-car smell goes away, and you are left with 57 months of car payments. You felt so good when you bought it, but now it doesn't feel so good (or smell so good, either, as a matter of fact).

Even smart people spend their money on stupid stuff.

Most people have a spending problem but blame other reasons for the fact they never have any money—the water heater broke, one of their kids needs braces, the dog swallowed a tennis ball and had to have emergency surgery. They continue to kid themselves, pretending that there isn't a problem with their spending and coping with it in their own way.

*Most people confuse the things they **want** with the things they **need**.*

To fix a problem, you first have to accept that there is one. If you continue to kid yourself and say you have a handle on your spending, you will always stay in the predicament you are currently in.

DOLLARS & UNCOMMON SENSE

In the same way that an alcoholic or a gambler needs to stand up and admit to their harmful behavior, you have to acknowledge you have a spending problem.

This step is usually the hardest. But once you have accepted the fact that, like most people, you have a problem with spending, you will be on the right track to changing the way you think about money and what you do with it. So how do you get to the point of acknowledging that you have a problem? You take a good, long look at just how much money you are spending and what you are spending it on.

Most people have no idea what, where, when, and how much they spend. What would you call someone who had no idea where their kids were, who they were with, or when they were getting home? A bad parent! The same goes with you and your money. If you have no idea what you are spending your money on, where it goes, and how much you spend, that makes you bad with money. Do not take it personally, but it is the truth.

This book will pay for itself many times over if you do what I tell you next.

For 31 days, I want you to start keeping receipts and writing down every time you spend your money. That's the only way to know where your money is going. It doesn't get any simpler than that. I will repeat it again: To know what, where, when, and how much you are spending, you have to keep receipts and write your spending down.

In the worksheets at the back of the book, you will find a blank Spending Tracker to fill out. On the top are the numbers 1 through 31. What do they represent? Yes, the days of the month.

PRINCIPLE: IF YOU SPEND LESS, YOU WILL HAVE MORE

Table 3-1a. Example of a Spending Tracker—blank

Item	1	2	3	4	5	6	etc.	31

Under the "Item" heading, write down what you spent your money on, and in the column for that day of the month, write how much you paid for that item. For example, let's say you start tracking your expenses on the third of the month. On your way to work, you stop by a fast-food restaurant to get a breakfast sandwich, and then to fill your tank with gas. You will write that spending down like this:

Table 3-1b. Example of a Spending Tracker—first day

Item	1	2	3	4	5	6	etc.	31
Breakfast			$6.22					
Gas			$25.00					

The next day, you follow the same morning ritual of getting a fast-food breakfast. You don't need gas, but at lunchtime you pay your cell phone bill. Your Spending Tracker will now look like this:

Table 3-1c. Example of a Spending Tracker—second day

Item	1	2	3	4	5	6	etc.	31
Breakfast			$6.22	$6.22				
Gas			$25.00					
Cell Phone Bill				$102.50				

You will continue writing down every time you spend money for a month. If you do, after 31 days you should have at least $150 to $250 more in your bank account than normal. The question is: How?

After 31 days you should have at least $150 to $250 more in your bank account than normal.

Have you ever had an annoying habit that you didn't realize you had until someone pointed it out? Once that annoying habit was made known to you, you probably quit or at least made a conscious effort to stop doing it. The same concept works when you write down every time you spend your money. You will begin to notice where you can start cutting some of your spending.

For instance, everybody needs food, but a lot of people could spend less by just eating out less. When you see how much you're spending on that fast-food breakfast every morning, you might decide to start grabbing something from your kitchen as you head out the door for work. If lunch is a big chunk of your spending, you might start packing your lunch three days a week. Or perhaps you get to the end of the first week and see that you are spending a lot on going out to dinner, so you decide to pick one night a week to go out instead of going out on Friday, Saturday, and Sunday night.

I know it might not always be possible to stop what you're doing and write down your spending right then and there, so keep a receipt for every single thing you buy that month. At the end of each day, go through your receipts and be sure to write down on your Spending Tracker every cent you spent. Try not to go longer than a day between writing down your spending. The longer you leave it, the more difficult it is to keep track; and if you keep an eye on your spending every day, you will save more money over the course of the month.

Be certain to use accurate, detailed information. For example, if you pull $50 out of the ATM, don't write down that you pulled out $50. Write down *exactly* where that $50 went. I remember that on many weekends when I was younger, I would withdraw $200 on a Friday night and end up looking in my wallet on Monday morning to find it empty. I had no idea where it went. You will have no idea where your money is going, either, unless you keep a receipt every time you spend, and then record it on your Spending Tracker. For now, you need to track your spending for just one month. If you find later on that your spending is starting to get out of whack, do this 31-day exercise again, and you will soon be back on track.

After you have written down your expenses for 31 days, your next steps are:

1. Put each expense into one of the eight categories below.
2. Add up your monthly totals.
3. Work out what percentage of your monthly paycheck you spent on each category.

Table 3-2 gives an example of an average person who takes home $3,000 a month net of taxes and health insurance.

Table 3-2. Example of a Spending Summary

Spending Category	Current Spending	
Giving		
	0.00	
Total Giving	0.00	0.0%
Saving		
	0.00	
Total Saving	0.00	0.0%
Housing		
Mortgage/Rent	775.00	
Homeowner's/Renter's Insurance	40.00	
Electricity	90.00	
Gas/Heating Oil	15.00	
Water and Sewer	50.00	
Home Telephone (Landline)	35.00	
Cell Phone	75.00	
Cable/Satellite Television	100.00	
Internet Fees	50.00	
Total Housing	1,230.00	41.0%

PRINCIPLE: IF YOU SPEND LESS, YOU WILL HAVE MORE

Food		
Groceries	300.00	
Breakfasts Out	25.00	
Lunches Out	75.00	
Dinners Out	200.00	
Quick Stops (Coffee, Snacks)	50.00	
Vending Machines	15.00	
Total Food	665.00	22.2%
Transportation		
Car Loan Payments	300.00	
Fuel and Oil	125.00	
Car Insurance	70.00	
Car Repairs	35.00	
Car Washes	10.00	
Total Transportation	540.00	18.0%
Clothing		
Self	25.00	
Spouse	75.00	
Children	50.00	
Dry Cleaning	40.00	
Total Clothing	190.00	6.3%
Debt Payments		
Credit Card Payments	125.00	
Personal Loan Payments	30.00	
Total Debt Payments	155.00	5.2%
Personal		
Medicines	30.00	
Life Insurance	30.00	
Music (CDs and downloads)	25.00	
Movies and DVD Rental and Purchase	30.00	
Alcoholic Beverages	25.00	
Gifts (Birthday, Graduation)	25.00	

Pets	30.00	
Hobbies	65.00	
Total Personal Spending	260.00	8.7%
Grand Total	$3,040.00	101.3%

I want to point out that this person is spending more money than they are making!

There is a blank version of this worksheet, titled Spending Summary, at the back of the book for you to fill in. Make sure you list where you spent your money under one of the eight categories, because this summary is going to be important when you put your Spending Plan together in Chapter 5. But before we do that, in the next chapter we're going to talk about resetting your priorities, because they will be integral to your plan.

THE TAKE HOME

- You spend because it makes you feel good in the short term. People who have money think *long term*.
- It is a misconception that making more money will help you have more money. Unless you change your spending habits, you will continue to spend more than you make.
- If you spend less, you will have more money.
- Don't confuse the things you *want* with the things you *need*.
- For the next 31 days, keep your receipts. Every time you

spend money, write it down on the Spending Tracker worksheet at the back of the book.

- At the end of the 31 days, add up your totals for giving, saving, shelter, food, transportation, clothing, debt payments, and personal expenses, and record them on the Spending Summary worksheet.

4: Priorities: Give, Pay Yourself, Pay Everybody Else

When I was a boy, I liked to play with my G.I. Joe action figures. My favorite Joe was the one with the orange beard and Kung-Fu Grip. My sister for some reason didn't like to play with her Barbie dolls but wanted to play with my G.I. Joes instead. Even though I had three G.I. Joes to play with, I didn't want to give any of them to my sister. I remember that she told on me for not sharing my toys with her and my mother screaming at me that if I didn't give my sister one of those G.I. Joes, she would take them all from me!

People are inherently greedy, and there is only one cure for greed: giving. How do parents teach their kids not to be greedy? They tell them to share with others. My mother was teaching me at an early age that it is good to give.

When we grow up and start spending our paychecks, many of us forget those lessons our parents taught us. Greed dominates most people's spending, because it makes them feel good in the short term. But because it encourages overspending and stops us from saving for the future, it impacts adversely on our financial health in the long term. Giving, which is the antidote to greed, barely features in most people's financial priorities. Most people:

1. Give money to causes rarely.
2. Don't save enough.[5]
3. Spend almost everything they make and live paycheck to paycheck.[6]

If you want more money, you have to change your priorities. You need to:

1. Give away 10 percent of what you make.
2. Save 10 percent.
3. Live on the rest.

Plenty of people have probably told you before that you need to "pay yourself first" by saving at least 10 percent of what you make. Don't get me wrong: I believe that saving at least 10 percent of what you make is crucial to your long-term financial health. You must do that. It's just that I believe *giving* 10 percent should be your number one priority, because it's the easiest and quickest way for you to start having more money. I know that sounds weird, but bear with me.

> *Giving away 10 percent of what you make is the easiest and quickest way for you to start having more money.*

---

5   In December 2010, Americans' rate of saving had increased from previous years, but we were still saving only 5 percent of our income, which is about half of what we need to be saving. Neil Irwin, "Climbing Out of Debt, Americans Are Saving More," *The Washington Post*, February 15, 2011.
6   In a 2010 study, 77 percent of American workers reported that they were living paycheck to paycheck. Study conducted by Harris Interactive© on behalf of CareerBuilder.com among 2,534 U.S. hiring managers and 4,498 U.S. workers, May–June 2010.

I don't have any agenda here: I am not telling you whom to give your money to. It could be a local soup kitchen, a school, someone in your community who is having trouble paying their medical bills, your church, an international aid organization, or a home for orphaned ferrets—whatever cause is important to you. All I care about is that you give first, and you give at least 10 percent. I will say it again: I don't care whom you give to! You just need to give 10 percent of what you make, and you need to do that before you do anything else with your paycheck. (For those of you who are already tithing 10 percent to your church first before you spend anything else, you can consider this priority covered.)

I already know what you are thinking. Using common sense, you're saying to yourself, "That's ridiculous! How can I have more money if I'm giving it away?"

This strategy works on numerous levels. First, if you are like most people and spend your whole paycheck every month without giving or saving, when you reset your priorities and start giving away 10 percent and then saving 10 percent, you will have 20 percent less money to live on. Very soon you will learn that you *can* survive on less. You will learn to be less materialistic, and you will become far more careful about your spending. And as we know from the previous chapter, the key to having more money is to save more and spend less. In addition, you will begin to grow savings, which you can use in an emergency, such as a major

*Very soon you will learn that you **can** survive on less.*

car or house repair, instead of maxing out another credit card or having your whole paycheck swallowed up in one hit.

The giving strategy works at a deeper level as well. Re-prioritizing

45

helps you begin to transform the way you think about money. If you truly want to change and succeed at building wealth, you have to think and act differently than most people. You do not want to be like everybody else and suffer from the spending disease. If you want things to be different, you have to do different things.

When I was going through basic training, my mind and body would tell me one thing ("This is agony, lie down and curl up into a ball") and the drill sergeant would be screaming something else ("Give me 10"). The sooner I quit fighting my natural tendencies, the quicker I was able to transform my old way of thinking into a new way of thinking. You are transforming the way you think about money into the way you need to think about money, so it's time to start using some *uncommon* sense instead.

*It's time to start using some **uncommon** sense instead.*

One of the 6 Key Traits of Wealth Builders that I have identified in my clients is that they do not let their emotions play a role in their financial decision making. If you truly want to change the way you think and be successful, you have no other option but to learn how to manage your emotions. Some money decisions will make you uncomfortable and won't feel natural. At first, giving 10 percent away will probably feel that way. But soon you will get used to it, it will stop feeling uncomfortable, and you will see that it increases the amount of money you have quickly and easily.

REAL-LIFE EXAMPLES

I want to share two stories of clients of mine who follow my advice to give away 10 percent before doing anything else with their money. My first story is about a couple who own an extremely successful heating and air-conditioning company in Monroe, North Carolina. They were not always successful. Both of them came from humble beginnings, and neither of their families had any money. He started out serving his country in the Army for a few years. After leaving the military, he wanted to start a business. He had an interest in heating and air-conditioning, so he and his wife started their business out of their garage, in 1981. They struggled at the beginning, like most young couples. But before all else, they would always give, even when doing so meant that they would have to do without. They both believe in hard work and sacrifice, and over the years they have built their business up to a multi-million-dollar corporation. To tell you the truth, I am not nearly as impressed by how successful they are in business as I am by the fact that they gave early on, when they had nothing.

One of the most stressful situations for a couple is when they are dealing with a lot of credit card debt. My next story is about a couple who racked up more credit card debt than I did when I was in the Army. In my experience, most couples do not see eye to eye when it comes to money. Usually one is more interested or concerned, and the other couldn't care less. In this case, the wife was a good saver, but the husband was an even better spender. Over the years, the husband racked up a tremendous amount of credit card debt. I really felt bad for the wife, because I could see the anguish in her eyes every time we had a meeting.

The wife finally could not handle the stress any longer and wanted to liquidate almost all of her retirement account to pay off a big chunk of their credit card debt. I told her it was a bad idea for two big reasons. The first was that she was in her 40s, which meant that when she took the money out of her retirement account, she would be penalized 10 percent for an early withdrawal and the money would be taxed. Depending on the state you live in and your tax bracket, unless you qualify for an exception, if you take money out of a retirement account prior to age 59½, after the taxes and penalties, you get approximately 55 cents on the dollar. Secondly, I knew that there was an even better reason not to pull that money out: I have said a million times that it isn't the money you have but the money you spend that gets you in trouble.

She went against my recommendations and used most of her retirement savings to pay off the debt. She and her husband treated the symptoms of credit card debt but didn't treat the underlying problem, which was that the husband loved to spend money. I am sorry to say that within a few years they were in the same predicament. This time, the wife finally got fed up and filed for divorce. To make things worse, the debt was in both of their names, even though it was her husband who caused them to get back into debt. According to the divorce decree, the wife accepted half of the debt in exchange for being able to keep all of the retirement money she was able to build back up.

The entire time, even when things were at their worst, the wife always gave 10 percent of what she made. Even though the marriage ended in a divorce, I have never seen her happier. She and her daughters are living on one income, but she continues to give 10 percent before she spends her money anywhere else. When we meet, she tells me things get tight at the end of the month, but they somehow have enough, even after she gives and puts a little money away for the future. The best part is that she will have her half of the credit card debt paid off in the next year or so. Her husband, on the other hand, never gave.

Can I explain how it works? No! I am just telling you that if you want to spend less, then you need to give first. I also believe that if you give, you will receive. I can't make it any simpler.

This is so contrary to what you read in the paper or see on TV, or how your neighbors and coworkers and friends live. We live in a culture of instant gratification. People believe that money will buy them happiness. Money might rent it for a while, but it won't provide you true happiness. Money only gives you choices.

Changing your spending priorities will mean making some sacrifices now, but I know it will make things better for you later. You *can* live on less, and when you prove that to yourself, you will actually have more money. Though it may feel strange at first, it will quickly become part of how you live your life. You will do this because you no longer want to be like most people.

To prove how effective this strategy is, test it out. For the next three months, when you receive your paycheck, give 10 percent, save 10 percent, and then live off the rest. You will see that you can live on less—and that you will end up with more. In the next chapter, we will go step-by-step through how to plan your spending to achieve this.

THE TAKE HOME

- Giving away 10 percent of what you make is the easiest and quickest way to start to have more money.
- If you want more money, you have to change your priorities. You need to:

1. Give away 10 percent of what you make.
2. Save 10 percent of what you make.
3. Live on the rest.

- Very soon you will learn that you *can* survive on less. You will become far more careful about your spending.

- Test out these new priorities for the next three months. Because the key to having more money is to save more and spend less, you will soon find that you have more money.

5: Plan: A Plan for Your Paycheck

Picture this: You're going to a party across town, at a house you've never been to before. For you to achieve that goal, you might go online and search your favorite map site, or plug the address into your GPS, or ask the host of the party for directions. No matter which of those options you choose, you need to know from where you will be starting your journey. The same is true with financial planning. In order to plan how to reach a financial goal, you need to know where you are starting from. That is why I got you to keep receipts and write down every time you spent money for 31 days, and complete the Spending Summary. Now you know where you are starting from.

Your goal is to:
- Give 10 percent of what you make away.
- Save 10 percent.
- Live on the rest.

For example, let's say you take home $3,000 after taxes and health insurance. You will give away 10 percent of $3,000, which is $300. I know how tough it will be for you to give your hard-earned money away, but you will be surprised by how different your financial outlook will be if you quit relying on your natural instincts, or common sense. You need to do the opposite of most people. You will never have more money unless you do.

I know how tough it will be for you to give your hard-earned money away.

After you have given your first 10 percent away, you will save 10 percent. Since we already know that 10 percent of $3,000 is $300, you will need to save at least $300 from your take-home pay each month. You work extremely hard for your money, so after giving, you need to pay yourself before you pay anybody else. That is what saving is: paying yourself.

And guess what you can do with the rest? You can spend it. This chart is a guideline for how to allocate your money each month.

Table 5-1. Monthly spending guidelines as a percentage of income

Giving	10%
Saving	10%
Housing	30–40%
Food	10–15%
Transportation	15–20%
Clothing	5–10%
Debt Payments	5–10%
Personal	10–15%

I'd like you to refer back to the Spending Summary I asked you to do in Chapter 3. Compare the percentage of your take-home pay that you spent on each category with the percentage you *should* be spending. This will give you a broad indication of where you need to cut spending.

Now let's move on to the specifics. Throughout, I will continue to use the $3,000-a-month take-home pay example, but remember that the same principles apply no matter how much you are making. The actual dollar amounts are not what's important—all that matters is that you allocate the right percentage of your paycheck to the eight spending categories. To draw up your own Spending Plan, use the worksheet at the back of the book.

THE 8 SPENDING CATEGORIES

Giving: 10 percent
As I said before, I don't care what cause or needy individual you give to, just make giving 10 percent your number one priority.

Saving: 10 percent
After giving, pay yourself 10 percent before you pay anybody else. In Parts 3 and 4, we will be looking at saving in depth.

Housing: 30–40 percent
The greatest percentage of your income, up to 40 percent, can be allocated to housing expenses, such as mortgage or rent, utilities, and repairs. That is a total of $1,200 a month based on an income of $3,000 a month.

If you are spending more than 40 percent of your take-home pay on housing, you need to see where you can start cutting. See if you can bring your utility bills down. If you have cable with 5,000 channels, with the premium-plus package, cut it down to basic cable or get rid of cable altogether. I remember when I was stationed in Suwon, South Korea, and I had the Armed Forces Network, which provided a total of three channels. Guess what? I survived.

Another expense you can reduce is your telephone bill. If you have a landline and a cell phone, consider getting rid of the landline. If you have the GPS, 1,000 minutes, unlimited text, and unlimited data cell-phone package, consider reducing it to the bare minimum. You can turn down the thermostat a few degrees during the wintertime and turn it up a few degrees during the summertime. You can also turn the thermostat on your water heater down a few degrees.

You need to set your own priorities. I just wanted to give you some ideas where you can maybe reduce your spending. If cable is really important to you, then find something else you can cut. But do not say, "I will just cut my giving." Don't cut your saving, either. Those are the first two places where your money needs to go, before it goes anywhere else.

What I'm about to say may sound extreme, but it works. If you're having trouble deciding what you can live without, go through the list of what you spend your money on, and item by item, ask yourself the following question: "If I was homeless, would I need _____?" I promise that you would not need cable if you were homeless, because you wouldn't have a TV or electricity. So before you say you can't live without something that you're currently spending money on each month, just think for a second.

Let's assume the worst-case scenario: You have already cut

back all your housing expenses to the bare essentials, and you are still spending more than 40 percent of your income on housing. Your next step would be to cut your spending in other categories, such as food, transportation, or clothing. Again, what I'm about to say may not be comfortable for you to hear, but it's the truth: If you are spending more than 40 percent of your monthly income on housing, that should be a big red flag screaming that you are in a house you can't afford. It is time to consider moving. In the short term, you aren't going to feel so good about moving, but in the

If you are spending more than 40 percent of your monthly income on housing, that should be a big red flag screaming that you are in a house you can't afford.

long term you will be better off. I am not going to lie to you and say these decisions are easy, but I can tell you that if you spend within the percentages I've allocated for each category every month, you will have more money.

Food: 10–15 percent

You should spend no more than 10–15 percent of your income on food. On a $3,000 income, that means you could spend up to about $112 a week on groceries and eating out. If you are spending more than $450 on food a month, you need to start considering eating out less often. For those who say they can't cook and that is the reason they go out so much, this is the only time I would ever recommend this: Consider spending a little more money in the housing category and purchase the cooking channels. I promise, it is a lot cheaper to learn how to cook than to go out to eat every night!

Transportation: 15–20 percent

I always joke that the nicest cars in a town with a military base usually belong not to doctors and lawyers and businesspeople but to G.I.s. When I was in the military and lived on post, there would always be some really nice cars parked outside. I had a friend who had this awesome ride that was always parked outside the barracks in the same spot day after day. One day I finally asked my friend if that was his favorite spot or something, and he told me that he was able to afford only the car payment and insurance. He didn't have any money left for gas.

You don't have to be in the military to appreciate that story. Everybody wants to keep up with the Joneses. They want the biggest house, nicest car, most expensive clothes, and to think they are living the life. You shouldn't be spending more than 20 percent of your income on transportation, or $600 a month based on a $3,000 income. That $600 must include car loan payments, gas, insurance, taxes, licenses, registration, and maintenance, or bus and train fares.

If you are like my friend in the military and have a flashy car you can't afford to drive, it's time to trade it in for something more affordable. Perhaps your family could even get by with one fewer car than you have. Try saving on gas by carpooling, walking, or taking a bus or train whenever possible.

Clothing: 5–10 percent

When it comes to clothes, people fall into one of two categories: They really love spending money on clothes, or they could not care less about clothes. For those who love buying new clothes all of the time, you are going to have to get used to spending between 5 and

10 percent of your monthly income on clothes. If you earn $3,000 a month, you can spend between $150 and $300 a month.

I like going clothes shopping more than my wife does. When I was younger, I could eat forever and not gain any weight. As I got older, I would gain weight just looking at food. I started having two sets of clothes: my skinny clothes for the summer and my not-so-skinny clothes for the winter. Around spring, I would spend a little more time at the gym to get my winter weight off. Last year, I did not get my winter weight off, and I was too big even for my winter clothes, let alone my summer skinny clothes. I have found out that it is a lot cheaper to eat better and exercise than it is to have to buy a whole bunch of new clothes because you can't fit into the ones in your closet!

Debt Payments: 5–10 percent

The debt I am talking about in this category is credit card, charge card, personal loan, and similar types of debt. Mortgage debt is separate, coming under the category of housing. Car loans fall under the category of transportation.

I really hate to allocate a percentage to debt. By saying that 5–10 percent of your income should be allocated to debt, I do not mean to imply that it is okay to keep racking up consumer debt. The reason that I include it in the plan for your paycheck is because in reality most people have some type of consumer debt.

In Part 3, we will be going into detail about debt, so for now I just want to tell you about two measures of debt that are helpful to know. Banks use these ratios for deciding how much of a house mortgage you can afford, but these concepts can also help you decide how to spend your money.

The first one is the *front-end ratio*. As a general rule, your monthly mortgage payment—which includes principal, interest, real estate taxes, and homeowner's insurance—should not be greater than 28 percent of your monthly income. Using the front-end ratio, the most a bank would let you borrow if you earned $3,000 a month would be a mortgage with repayments totaling no more than $840 a month.

The *back-end ratio* is a measure of your total amount of debt ob-ligations, including your house mortgage, car loans, credit cards, student loans, lines of credit, and any other debts you might have. In order for the bank to lend you money, the total amount you are paying toward all of these debts combined can't be greater than 36 percent of your monthly income. Multiply $3,000 × 0.36 and you get $1,080, which would be the maximum the bank would allow you to borrow.

> *If you want a bigger house, then you need to have a smaller car payment. If you'd rather have a nicer car, then guess what? You need to have a smaller house.*

What these ratios show us is that if you want a bigger house, then you need to have a smaller car payment or have your credit cards paid off. If you'd rather have a nicer car, then guess what? You need to have a smaller house, so that all your ratios stay where they should be. I can't tell you which purchases are most important to you, but if you want more money, you have to spend less. That might mean living in a smaller house, driving an older car, not wearing the latest designer clothes, or cutting back on whatever you are currently going into debt to pay for.

Personal: 10–15 percent

I believe you work hard and should be rewarded. I do not live in a fairy-tale world where I think you won't spend money on anything but the bare essentials of food, housing, clothing, and transportation. I also don't want you to feel stressed out and pressured because you think that you can't spend a little money on yourself. What I am saying is that if you want more money, you have to spend less, so you need to keep your personal spending within limits. I recommend spending 10–15 percent of your monthly income on personal and recreational things such as haircuts, going to the beauty salon, buying magazines, going to the movies, and hobbies. Other items I would also include in this category are health- and life-insurance premiums. I really think that you *should* spend some money on yourself, and that if you are married, you should allow your spouse to as well. Let me share the following story.

> *I don't want you to feel stressed out and pressured because you think that you can't spend a little money on yourself.*

Two pretty funny clients of mine are a husband and wife who have no problem arguing and making mean faces at each other in front of me. The first few times we met, I felt a little uncomfortable with their shenanigans, but as time passed, I got used to it. Both of them work very hard and make pretty good money. He loves spending money, and she loves saving money. When they went over their monthly budget each month, they would always end up in a big fight about his spending, so they made an appointment to come see me for help. I knew how both of them were thinking before they even came in: She expected me to tell him to quit

59

spending so much, and he expected me to tell him to quit spending so much.

I had a plan when they came in. I told them I wanted to talk with each of them by themselves first, and then I would talk with them together. I sat down with the wife first and told her to give her husband an allowance. She looked at me as if I had a third eye in the middle of my forehead. So I asked her if there was ever a time when she was a teenager that her parents forbade her from going out with a boy. She said yes. I asked her, "How did that make you feel?" She said that it made her want to go out with that guy even more. Once she said that, I could see a lightbulb click on in her mind. I explained, "If you tell your husband not to spend any money, it will only make him want to spend more. Let him spend 3 percent of what you both make on anything he wants, and do not question him. I bet things will go smoother." I asked her to step out and let me speak with her husband.

Before he had a chance to say anything, I asked him whether he would be happy if he could spend $250 a month on anything he wanted and his wife wouldn't say anything. He just looked at me like I was crazy. I asked him again, "Would you be happy?" He nodded his head yes.

I then had them both come in together to go over the plan. As they did their spending plan each month, they would allocate 3 percent of what they made to a special account. I told him that he could spend whatever was in the account but couldn't spend any more. About three months later, the wife called me up to thank me and say they were no longer fighting over money.

When someone tells you "No" or "You can't," it is human nature to put up some resistance. I always say, "There should be a little give and take." I would never recommend that you have to save every dollar you make in order to have more money. I am just telling you that the only way that you will ever have more money is by spending less. You will never learn to spend less unless you learn how to give first. You will also never have any money unless you save some of it. For those reasons, I don't give any wiggle room on the first two spending priorities, giving and saving. But once you have set aside 10 percent for each of those, you can have some flexibility about how you spend the rest of your money, which is why I have given percentage ranges, such as 30–40 percent and 5–10 percent. As an example, perhaps you prefer to spend the full 40 percent on housing, because you feel you can get by spending the minimum on clothing and personal expenses. Balance your spending the way that works best for you, while staying within the guidelines.

PUTTING THE PLAN IN MOTION

Now is the time to apply what you have learned. Choose the day that you are going to start tracking every time you spend money. After tracking your spending for 31 days, pick a day or two when you know you will have some spare time to put your spending in the correct categories. Once you have completed that, the next part will be the hardest and most time-consuming. Since I gave you only a range, you will have to make your own priorities. For example, if you prefer to have a bigger house, you will need a smaller car, so you will have to adjust your percentages accordingly. Go through each category and determine how you are going to keep your spending within the recommended percentage ranges.

The next part of the plan will be less of a pain in your butt than it may sound at first:

I recommend that you open additional accounts for bills that are due less frequently than every month. Let's assume your car insurance costs $600 every six months. You will put $100 each month into a car-insurance account, so at the end of six months you will have the money you need to pay the bill. The same goes for your vacation fund. You will open another account, and each month you will put a little into it, so when it is time for vacation, you won't have to charge it.

Why am I telling you this? When I was a boy, I was always told to make sure my plate was clean after supper. I think many other kids were told the same thing. Unfortunately, most of us do the same thing with our paycheck: For some reason, we act as though we have to spend all of the money we make. I can remember many times in my younger days, in the Army, when my checking account was down to the cents. If you feel as though you have to spend everything you make, then I strongly, strongly, strongly recommend that you open multiple accounts. If you keep everything in one account, you are likely to spend everything in that account.

A lot of people do not buy clothes every month but basically shop twice a year, usually for summer and winter. If you only go clothes shopping twice a year and always use a charge card when you do, open yourself a clothes account. Each month, put up to 5 percent of your income in that account, and at the end of six months, you can shop to your heart's content, as long as you spend only what you have in your clothes account and no more.

If you find that you are weak in any one of the spending categories, just open a separate account for it. Either write checks and pay them into your separate savings accounts once a month, or do electronic drafts. I do not care which method you choose. I just want you to change the way you have been handling your money, because what you have done in the past is not working. Do something different!

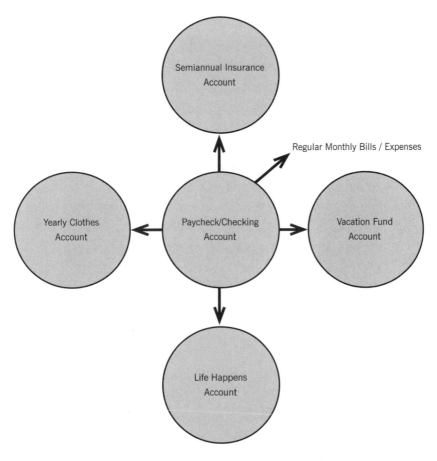

Figure 5-1. Open separate accounts so you don't spend everything you earn.

THE TAKE HOME

- When you get paid, make a spending plan for that month, allocating a percentage of your total paycheck to each of the 8 Spending Categories.
- The 8 Spending Categories are:
    Giving: 10 percent
    Saving: 10 percent
    Housing: 30–40 percent
    Food: 10–15 percent
    Transportation: 15–20 percent
    Clothing: 5–10 percent
    Debt Payments: 5–10 percent
    Personal: 10–15 percent
- For special spending, problem spending, or bills that are paid less frequently than once a month, open up separate accounts and pay money into the accounts each month, just as you would pay any other monthly expenses.

Part 3

Debt

6: Principle: Debt Puts Your Financial Health at Risk

Debt is worse than a four-letter word. Debt is a disease. It is a very contagious disease, because there are so many people who have it. You have the disease if you can tick one or more of these boxes:

- ☐ I can afford to make only the minimum payments toward my debts each month.
- ☐ I use credit cards to make everyday purchases because I have no money in my checking and savings accounts.
- ☐ Twenty percent or more of my take-home pay is going toward paying debt (other than a home mortgage or car loan payment).
- ☐ I am making my credit card payments with other credit cards.
- ☐ Most or all of my credit cards are maxed out, and I am trying to get additional credit.

You didn't get into debt up to your eyeballs overnight. You didn't just wake up one morning with all of your credit cards maxed out and wondering how you had accumulated so much debt. Most likely you started accumulating debt during the early years of your adult life. You were probably single and weren't worrying about the future; you definitely weren't thinking about the pressure that debt would put you under later in life.

For most people, the story then goes like this: They get married, carrying debt over from their old single life into their new marriage. Often they think that because their spouse is working, they can start to count on the extra income to help pay off debts—when in reality their spouse is probably in debt, so now they have double the debt.

Excuse after excuse, they continue getting further and further in debt. Then they have children. They didn't make paying off debt a priority early on in their marriage, and now they have more mouths to feed and even less money to pay toward their debts. The pressure is overwhelming. It affects people's health, peace of mind, marriages, and their relationships with their kids. I can certainly tell you that it puts their financial health at risk.

The story of the average person in debt may not be exactly yours. Perhaps you're still young or single, or you don't have kids. But if you ticked any of the boxes above, then I know you can tell some version of the debt story. Now I want to tell you my story. I left the Army after 12 years of service with $32,000 worth of credit card debt. It didn't happen overnight. It started off small. When I was a private, I got my

I left the Army after 12 years of service with $32,000 worth of credit card debt.

first credit card. The maximum I could charge was $500. I was so excited knowing that someone was going to give me $500.

That is how I thought—that someone was *giving* me $500. I knew I had to pay it back eventually, but I actually thought the bank was doing me this great big favor letting me charge so much. After my first promotion, the bank rewarded me again, by raising the maximum that I could charge to $1,000. After two years, I was making more money, and the bank sent me a letter saying that the maximum I could charge was $2,000.

Then one day, I opened the mailbox and I had an offer from another bank wanting me to use their card. I remember reading that when my application was approved, they could offer me up to $2,000. I got dizzy just thinking about all the stuff that I could buy with $2,000. I had already maxed out my first credit card with the $2,000 balance. I was approved for the second card, and within a few weeks, my credit card debt had doubled to $4,000.

All the time I was denying that I was financially sick. I thought to myself that as long as I could pay the minimums on my credit cards each month, everything was okay. Each year the pattern continued. I would get a promotion, the bank would increase my maximum, and then I would max out my cards. Then one day I got smarter.

All the time I was denying that I was financially sick.

I understood that it would be better to pay a lower interest rate, so I started applying for other credit cards that didn't charge as much interest. Lucky me, I received another offer from a bank. They were going to charge me only 20 percent instead of the 24 percent I was currently paying, and they would approve me moving $3,500 of my balance on the other cards over. That was such a smart move, I thought at the time. Then guess what? A few months later, I had three credit cards that were maxed out. As long as I continued to be promoted and made more money, I was able to pay my bills, and all along I thought everything was fine.

Fast-forward a few years: I was offered a 0 percent credit card balance transfer. I was older and smarter, and I knew that with a 0 percent balance transfer I could once and for all start paying off my credit card debt.

Not only did I max out my new 0 percent credit card, all my other ones were maxed out also. And even worse, the teaser rate expired and went from 0 percent to 18 percent. It wasn't until I got out of the Army that I learned my lesson. As long as banks continued to give me credit cards, shortly after that I would have maxed them out, so I would need to quit charging and start saving. Believe me, I understand how easy it is to get deeply in debt. The truth is, I may not have learned this lesson at all if I hadn't become a financial planner and realized I couldn't be giving advice to others when my personal finances were a mess! In the following chapters, I am going to show you the steps you need to take to get yourself out of debt once and for all. I know these steps work, because they are the same ones I took myself.

IS ALL DEBT BAD?

The truth is that there are a few instances where you might have no choice but to accumulate some debt. You may have heard a well-known financial guru say that he thinks you should not have *any* debt, including a home mortgage. I do not live in la-la land, so when I make recommendations, I try to give real-world advice. In reality, most people will not be able to save enough to purchase their first home with cash, so I believe that taking out a mortgage is acceptable. I do not recommend counting on your residence as your retirement plan or getting a 30-year mortgage in your 50s, but if you have to borrow for a home, then I won't get onto you for that. You should make it a goal to have your home paid off as soon as possible, though. If you do, you might be able to retire a few years earlier.

I do not live in la-la land, so when I make recommendations, I try to give real-world advice.

Education is another place where you might need to accumulate some debt. It would be nice if college was free, but most people are not truly needy and do not qualify for assistance. I recommend the pay-as-you-go route, but that is not an option for everybody. For some, there is no choice but to get student loans. I think it is never a bad idea to invest in an education. If I had to decide between going to school and having student loans or not going to school, I would choose going to school and having student loans. The real problem is that most young people are bombarded with offers for credit cards, so not only do they have student loan debt when they graduate and enter the workforce but also a bunch of consumer debt. As a parent, I strongly recommend talking to your kids about debt, just as you would tell them about the birds and the bees. You really don't want them to learn those lessons from somebody else!

Finally, another circumstance when it is not too terrible to have some debt is if you are starting a business, so long as you have done your research and are not taking on more risk than you can handle. With risk comes rewards, but not all risks are worth taking, so if you are going to borrow to start a business, do be cautious.

All other debt is bad, including car loans. Realistically, though, I understand that you might need to borrow money to purchase a car. If you do get a loan, I want you to at least consider this advice: Do not buy a new car. I already talked about how quickly the new-car smell fades, but new cars lose value even faster than that. Actually, they can lose thousands of dollars in value the instant you drive them out of the car dealership, because while you paid the retail price, the most the car is worth now is the wholesale price that the dealer would pay for it if you brought it back. A rule of thumb is that cars lose about 20 percent of their value every year.[7]

What I recommend is that you pick a car you like and find out what the monthly payments are, but don't buy the car. Instead, practice making your car payments for a year by placing them into a car savings account. After you have made monthly payments for a year into that account, go back and get a loan to buy the same model. It will be a year old, which means it will be cheaper, and you will also have a nice down payment. Think long term. Don't let the new-car smell entice you to make a purchase that might make you feel good in the short term, only to leave a bad taste in your mouth when you are left with six years of car payments.

The less debt you have, the more money you will have, so next we're going to look at how to take control of your debts, especially unacceptable forms of debt, such as credit cards.

---

7   Lucy Lazarony, "Know the Deal on Auto Depreciation," www.bankrate.com/brm/news/auto/20011226a.asp accessed May 26, 2011.

THE TRUE COST OF DEBT

Step one in taking control of your debt is realizing just how damaging it is to your financial (and physical and emotional) health. With credit card offers appearing every day in the mail and the whole world seemingly living on credit, it's easy to talk yourself into believing that it's okay to have several maxed-out credit cards and be making just the minimum payments each month. The truth is that debt is putting you at risk and is costing you more than you realize.

Debt is putting you at risk and is costing you more than you realize.

Case in point: If you put money in the bank, you might earn 0.5 percent interest if you are lucky, but if you borrow from that same bank, they will charge you 20 percent interest. If I gave you $1 and asked you to give me $20 in return, I doubt that you would want to make that deal. Yet this is what we do with banks all the time. You *cannot* make money when you are continuously repaying the bank $12 for every $10 you borrow. I always say, "It doesn't take a lot of money to make a lot of money," but you won't have any money if you are giving it to the credit card company. If you keep on accumulating debt, you will never get your chance to earn interest. Instead, you will always be paying it. You *can* make money, though, if you are earning interest on your savings.

I want to share with you an example of just how much your debt could be costing you. Let's pretend it's a week before the Super Bowl. You think to yourself, "Wouldn't it be nice to watch the game on a big-screen TV? While we're at it, let's throw in a surround-sound system so we can really enjoy the big game." You go down to your favorite retail store and charge the TV and a surround-sound system. You find them on sale. The total price with tax is $1,099. The minimum payment is only $25 a month, and the interest rate is 22 percent. You got yourself a pretty good deal, you think. When it's all said and done, you will have it paid off in seven years and seven months, and it will have cost you $2,256. If you'd had the cash, you could have bought yourself two big-screen TVs and two surround-sound systems for the price you ended up paying for one.

I have another example. The numbers vary depending upon where you do your research, but in 2006, according to the U.S. Census Bureau, Americans had more than $886 billion in credit card debt, and that figure was expected to rise to $1.177 trillion by the end of 2010. More specifically, the bureau reported that each card holder had an average credit card debt of $5,100, and this number was projected to reach $6,500 by the end of 2010.[8]

Let's assume the following: On one card you have a balance of $4,950. The interest rate is 22 percent, and you are making a monthly payment of $100. On another card, you have a balance of $1,850. The interest rate is a little better on the second card. You are only being charged 14 percent, and you are making a monthly payment of $30. If you don't charge anymore, you will have both of your credit cards paid off in *only* 11 years. The *only* part is a joke. That is really a long time. Not only will you be under this burden for more than a decade, you will end up paying $16,400, made up of the $6,800 you charged and $9,600 in interest.

---

8   Consumer Debt Statistics, Money-Zine.com, www.money-zine.com/Financial-Planning/Debt-Consolidation/Consumer-Debt-Statistics, accessed May 27, 2011.

I don't know about you, but I think I would rather keep that $9,600 instead of giving it to the credit card company. Let's assume that $9,600 was put into a hypothetical investment that earned an average of 10 percent for 11 years. It would grow to almost $27,400. A friendly reminder: People with little or no money think short term, and people with money think long term.

Do not let your mind try to justify that being in debt is fine. Your body manages to function even when it is infected by certain bad organisms and parasites, yet that doesn't mean that it is functioning well. Debt is a parasite that is sucking your financial health away. Do not kid yourself that as long as you are able to function, you are financially healthy. Don't tell yourself, "I'm able to make my minimum payments," "I don't have as much debt as my neighbor," or "I will pay my debt off by using my next bonus check or tax refund check." People make poor choices all the time because they believe they can manage the outcomes.

> *Debt is a parasite that is sucking your financial health away.*

The reason so many people are in debt is because it has become normal to us. This is especially the case with credit card debt. Just because it's normal doesn't make it healthy. Another reason people can't get out of debt is that they don't accept the truth that they will have to change their lifestyle and spending habits. Everybody *can* change, but nobody really wants to. Don't blame it on the bank or the credit card companies. It is your fault. You told yourself you needed this or that, and now you are on the hook. Stop getting any deeper in debt, and start *keeping* more of your hard-earned money. Don't stay in denial—it can be a killer.

Finally, whenever you are tempted to charge something, remember this: At the end of the day, if you don't outright own something, it does not belong to you. My best friend, Derrell, has always told me, "Don't love something that can't love you back." Your house will never love you. Your car will never love you. Things can't ever love you, though you may think you love them. Credit card companies do not love you, either.

Don't love something that can't love you back.

If you start making some short-term sacrifices now, those sacrifices will make you financially healthy in the long term.

THE TAKE HOME

- The only debts that can be considered beneficial are home mortgages, student loans, and business loans.
- Debt is putting you at risk and costing you more than you realize.
- The less debt you have, the more money you will have. You *cannot* make money when you are continuously paying the bank more in interest than you are earning from your savings.
- If you don't outright own something, it does not belong to you.
- Don't blame it on the bank or the credit card companies. It is your fault.
- Stop getting any deeper in debt, and start keeping more of your hard-earned money.

7: Priorities: Quit Charging and Start Saving

I heard someone joke, "If you can't live within your means, get more credit." I really didn't think it was that funny. People are hurting because of how much debt they are in. Too much debt messes up your credit; gives you a feeling of helplessness and stress; and puts your physical and emotional health at risk, let alone your financial health. More credit will not fix any of your problems; and I promise, you will never get out of debt if you continue to charge.

I think of debt like a drug. When a person charges something on their credit card, they feel better at that moment. As that spending high fades way, they look for their next fix. What ends up happening is that they need to spend more and more to feel good. Just like people who use drugs, they tell themselves they have a handle on their problem and that they're in control. That is how I thought when I had all of that credit card debt. The problem was that I woke up with a $32,000 hangover.

Debt is like a drug.

One of the hardest steps of getting out of debt is making it a top priority and keeping it there. Most people start off on the right track, just to get back in debt again, often worse than before. From now on, you will not let anything come before getting out of debt.

The cause of your debt is that you have a spending problem. If you try to blame it on anything else, you will forever be in debt. You will have to make some hard choices. If your choice is to take a vacation or work toward getting out of debt, you will have to make the hard choice and delay that vacation until you are out of debt or can pay for your vacation with cash.

QUIT CHARGING

The first step toward getting out of debt is to *quit dang charging*! You really do have to follow this rule if you ever want to get out of debt. Go ahead and pull out a pad of sticky notes and write "I will .... not charge any more!" on several, then stick them up *Quit dang* in places where they will be a constant reminder to *charging!* stop getting deeper into debt. Put those sticky notes on your bathroom mirror, your car visor, the door of your refrigerator, and any other places where you will see them often.

The next thing you are going to do is pull out a Tupperware bowl, fill it with water, put your credit cards in the bowl, and then put that bowl in the freezer. Standing around waiting for a great big ball of ice to melt will certainly give you the chance to think twice about whether you really do need to charge something. It might sound silly, but have you tried it? Start doing different things, and I promise that you will start getting different results. I am not joking: That is what you need to do. If you quit charging, I promise that you will finally begin to take control of your debt.

START SAVING

Before we go any further, I want to test your knowledge to see what you have learned so far. Take this hypothetical situation: You have $500 in your checking account, $100 in your savings account, and a credit card balance of $3,200. You earn no interest in your checking account and 0.5 percent interest in your savings account, and the credit card company is charging you 20 percent interest. It is May 10, and you just received a tax refund check for $1,800. What are you going to do?

Please don't tell me you are going to spend it.

All right, you would use it to pay down your credit card balance. It makes sense. *Wrong!* You should put $1,400 in your savings account and pay $400 toward your credit card balance.

I know how you are thinking: It doesn't make sense. Why would you put that much money into your savings and so little into the credit card when the bank is paying you only 0.5 percent and the credit card company is charging you 20 percent? Quit using common sense when dealing with your money. Start using some uncommon sense. The reason you would put that money into your savings account is because "life happens."

Let's assume you spend all of that tax refund check on paying down your credit card, leaving you with still only $100 in your savings account. And on May 11, the transmission goes out in your car. Or your water heater goes out. That's right, you will have no choice but to use your credit card, putting you right back at the same level of debt again—debt that you will have to pay 20 percent interest on. In the next chapter, we are going to plan step-by-step how to build up your savings for those "life happens" moments and then finally get rid of your debt.

THE TAKE HOME

- You will never get out of debt if you continue to charge, so quit dang charging!
- Write "I will not charge any more!" on sticky notes and place them where they will be a constant reminder.
- Freeze your credit cards inside a Tupperware bowl full of water.
- Start saving for emergencies so that you don't have to use your credit card and end up even more in debt.

8: Plan: Uncommon Sense Steps for Getting out of Debt

YOUR LIFE HAPPENS ACCOUNT
Once you start making a spending plan each month (see Chapter 5), you will begin spending less than what you are earning, and you will start to have more money. Common sense may tell you that to get on top of your debt, you should immediately use that extra money to start paying more than the minimum monthly payments on your debts. That is *not* what I want you to do. I want you to use uncommon sense instead and first focus on building up enough savings in a Life Happens Account to cover emergencies. That way, when you suddenly find out you need a root canal or your washing machine breaks and has to be replaced, you can cover that expense with cash rather than putting it on a credit card. *Saving is the only cure for debt, just as giving is the only cure for greed.* If you want to get out of debt, you have to save.

> *Saving is the only cure for debt, just as giving is the only cure for greed.*

You need to have $1,500 in your Life Happens Account. Some other financial books recommend that you should have at least $1,000 saved up. I have added an additional $500 because of inflation. You can take care of most emergencies if you have $1,500 in your Life Happens Account.

Right now you may be thinking that you'll be in debt forever if you have to wait until you've saved $1,500 to start paying more than the minimum payments on your credit cards. But it may take you much less time than you think. Let's say you have $0 in savings and that after making the minimum payments on your credit cards, you have $125 left over from your paycheck for the month. If you put that $125 a month in your savings, by the end of the year, you will have $1,500 in your Life Happens Account. If after making the minimum payments on your credit cards you can come up with $250 from your paycheck, it will take you only six months to save up $1,500 in your Life Happens Account. If you already have a little in savings, it will take you even less time.

Table 8-1. Time it takes to save $1,500 into your Life Happens Account

Amount You Save Each Month	When You Will Reach $1,500
$125	12 months
$250	6 months
$0	Never

I want to point out two important take homes: First, you should make only the minimum payments toward your credit cards until you have saved $1,500. Second, you should set a fixed minimum dollar amount that you will pay into your Life Happens Account each month. Think of it as your minimum monthly payment. If you have extra cash some months, pay more into your Life Happens

Account. The more you put in, the quicker you will reach the goal of having $1,500. If you have an emergency expense, draw on what you have saved in your Life Happens Account, and then start saving again until you have topped it back up to $1,500.

ASSESS YOUR DEBT

Once you have $1,500 in your Life Happens Account, it's time to get out of denial about your debt and make an honest assessment of the situation. This will give you the baseline you need in order to come up with the most effective, fastest payment plan to get out of debt. Using the Debt Assessor in the worksheets at the back of the book, write down each debt, the interest rate you are being charged, the outstanding balance, and how much you are paying each month. Then add up all the outstanding balances and all your total payments. For this example, let's say you have three credit cards and a total of $7,000 credit card debt, and you pay a total of $140 toward that debt each month.

Table 8-2. Example of a Debt Assessor worksheet

Debt	Interest Rate	Outstanding Balance	Minimum Payment
Credit Card A	14%	$1,000	$20
Credit Card B	19%	$3,500	$70
Credit Card C	22%	$2,500	$50
		$7,000	$140

Because for most people debt means credit card debt, I have used credit card balances in this and all the other examples in this chapter. The same principles apply for any type of debt you may have, such as student loans, personal loans, or department store payment plans. So when you assess your debt and plan your debt-payment strategy, include any such debts, not only credit card debts. You do not need to include your home mortgage or car payments, because you are already taking care of them under the categories of housing and transportation in your Spending Plan. Note that in all the examples in this chapter, I have assumed that each of the minimum monthly credit card payments is calculated using a payment of 2 percent of the outstanding balance.

PLAN TO BE DEBT FREE

The next step is to develop a plan, but first, I want to make an important assumption: *You are not going to charge anything else or borrow any more.*

There are a few different ways to pay off debt. Since this book is designed to help you have more money, I will show you the quickest and the most financially beneficial way.

First, I do not believe that credit consolidation is the answer. The same goes with personal bankruptcy. Credit consolidation or bankruptcy will treat the symptom but won't cure the true problem.

Credit consolidation or bankruptcy will treat the symptom but won't cure the true problem.

Think of the medicine you take to treat a cold. The medicine doesn't cure the cold; it just masks the symptoms. In the same way, if you consolidate your credit card debt into a home equity line of credit or other loan, or if you declare bankruptcy, you are treating only the symptom. What frequently happens is that your spending habits don't change, and then you have a maxed-out equity line *and* maxed-out credit cards. Debt is caused by a spending problem, and no matter what you do, if you spend more than what you make, you will always be in debt.

Second, I don't agree with the advice you often hear that you should pay the greatest amount of money toward the smallest balance. In my opinion, that is not the fastest way to get out of debt, nor is it the most financially beneficial way, unless the smallest balance is also the one with the highest interest rate. The people who recommend paying the greatest amount of money toward the smallest balance say it is a good thing because it can create a very motivating feeling of accomplishment. I am not concerned with how you might feel. My goal is to get you out of debt the fastest and most financially beneficial way. My viewpoint is that the worse you feel, the less likely it is you will ever want to be in credit card debt again. So my simple rule is to pay the greatest amount toward the debt with the highest interest rate. You can see how this works in the following example.

My goal is to get you out of debt the fastest and most financially beneficial way.

Table 8-3a. Example of a get-out-of-debt plan—the starting point

Debt	Interest Rate	Outstanding Balance	Minimum Payment
Credit Card A	14%	$1,000	$20
Credit Card B	19%	$3,500	$70
Credit Card C	22%	$2,500	$50
		$7,000	$140

Let's say that in your Spending Plan, you have allocated $200 toward your credit card debts. Your minimum payments come to $140 total. You will put the extra $60 toward the credit card with the highest interest rate. Which one is that? Correct, it's C. You will pay $20 toward Credit Card A, $70 toward Credit Card B, and $110 toward Credit Card C.

Table 8-3b. Example of a get-out-of-debt plan—stage 1

Debt	Interest Rate	Outstanding Balance	Minimum Payment	Your Plan
Credit Card A	14%	$1,000	$20	$20
Credit Card B	19%	$3,500	$70	$70
Credit Card C	22%	$2,500	$50	$110
		$7,000	$140	$200

You will continue to pay those amounts until Credit Card C is paid off. Then you will pay $180 toward Credit Card B, since it has the next-highest interest rate, and continue to pay $20 toward the card with the lowest interest rate.

Table 8-3c. Example of a get-out-of-debt plan—stage 2

Debt	Interest Rate	Outstanding Balance	Minimum Payment	Your Plan
Credit Card A	14%	$700	$20	$20
Credit Card B	19%	$2,900	$70	$180
Credit Card C	22%	$0	$0	$0
		$3,600	$90	$200

Once Credit Card B is paid off, you will pay $200 to Credit Card A, until it is paid off.

Table 8-3d. Example of a get-out-of-debt plan—stage 3

Debt	Interest Rate	Outstanding Balance	Minimum Payment	Your Plan
Credit Card A	14%	$420	$20	$200
Credit Card B	19%	$0	$0	$0
Credit Card C	22%	$0	$0	$0
		$420	$20	$200

I want to make an important point here: What usually happens is that when a person pays one debt off, they take that extra money and spend it. Let's look at what would happen if you just kept on making the minimum payments. As a reminder, here are the minimum payments again:

Table 8-4. Example of minimum monthly credit card payments

Debt	Interest Rate	Outstanding Balance	Minimum Payment
Credit Card A	14%	$1,000	$20
Credit Card B	19%	$3,500	$70
Credit Card C	22%	$2,500	$50
		$7,000	$140

If you make the minimum payments each month, you will have Credit Card A paid off first, after six years and four months. You will then have $20 you can do something else with. I would recommend that you take that $20 and add it to the debt with the highest interest, Credit Card C.

Instead, you act like most people and start spending that $20 instead of applying it toward your debt. You continue to pay $70 toward Credit Card B, and that card is paid off in eight years and four months. You start spending that $70 also and continue to pay only $50 toward Credit Card C, and you have that one paid off in 11 years and five months. On that $7,000 of total credit card debt you started off with, you ended up paying not only the $7,000, but also $8,338.40 in interest, for a grand total of $15,338.40!

This time, let's say that instead of spending that $20 when Credit Card A is paid off, you put that $20 toward the credit card with the highest interest rate, Credit Card C. You pay $70 toward Credit Card C and $70 toward Credit Card B. Once Credit Card B is paid off, you pay $140 toward Credit Card C until it, too, is paid off. By doing that, you are able to pay off your credit cards almost three years sooner and save about $600 in interest payments.

Now I want to challenge you. Go through your Spending Plan and see what you can either cut out or reduce so that you can come up with another $75 a month to put toward your debt. That is only about $2 a day! Using our example, that would mean that instead of paying $140 a month toward your credit card debt, you would pay $215. Paying off one credit card at a time and putting the extra money toward the credit card with the next-highest rate, you would save about $5,500 in interest payments and have all of your debt paid off in three years and 10 months, instead of 11 years and five months.

It's your choice.

You can pay $15,300 over the next 11 years and five months to a credit card company and have nothing to show for it, or you can pay off your credit cards in three years and 10 months, and then save the $215 you were using to pay your credit card debts each month. At the end of 11 years and five months, you would have close to $20,000 in the bank.

Fuzzy math? *No.*

By coming up with an additional $75 and adding it to the $140 you were already paying each month toward your debt, you would have your debt paid off in three years and 10 months, which is seven years and seven months earlier. That is 91 months earlier. If you saved that $215 for 91 months, you would have almost $20,000 saved up, because $91 \times \$215 = \$19,565$.

Take it from me. I had $32,000 worth of credit card debt that I was able to pay off by following the same steps I have shown you here. I won't lie to you and say that it was fun or easy, but I can tell you that I did it—and if I can, you can also!

I had $32,000 worth of credit card debt that I was able to pay off by following the same steps I have shown you here.

To develop your own get-out-of-debt plan, go to the following website: www.powerpay.org. It is a free site created through the cooperative efforts of Utah State University and WebAIM.org, neither of which I have any affiliation with. I really like it because you can develop a customized debt-reduction plan suited to you, and the great thing is that it won't cost anything except your time.

Something that might help you to stay out of trouble is to "opt out." Many companies prescreen potential customers based on their credit reports and then send out preapproved offers. To curb the temptation to get more credit and reduce the risk of identity theft, you can call 1-888-5-OPT-OUT (1-888-567-8688) or visit www.optoutprescreen.com to help reduce the number of unsolicited credit offers you receive.

So what do you do with your cards when you get them paid off? I do not recommend that you close the accounts, as that could affect your credit score. Either keep the cards in the Tupperware bowl that I had you place in the freezer, or just cut them up.

THE TAKE HOME

- Save $1,500 in your Life Happens Account.
- Assess your debt.
- Allocate most of your monthly debt payment toward the debt with the highest interest rate, and pay the minimums on the rest.
- Once a card is paid off, add the money you were paying on that card to the payment for the card with the next-highest interest rate. Keep doing this until all your debts are paid off.
- After all of your debt is paid off, you will start saving and investing what you were paying out to those credit card companies and start earning interest instead of paying interest.

Part 4
Saving and Investing

9: Principle: It Doesn't Take a Million to Make a Million

Imagine this situation. I ask a 21-year-old, "Do you have $1,800 that you can invest with me right now?" He tells me no. I then ask, "Can you save $150 a month?" He again tells me no. So I ask, "Are you wasting $5 a day?" He tells me yes, he is wasting $5 a day.

Saving $5 a day would add up to $150 a month, and by the end of the year it would add up to $1,800.

It is a lot easier to come up with $1,800 a year than what you think. And this is the best part: If $150 continued to be added to an investment every month for 20 years and compounded at a rate of 10 percent, when that 21-year-old was 65, the investment would have grown to $1,243,173. Yes, *more than $1.2 million*.[9]

---

9   It is important to remember that all scenarios are hypothetical examples of mathematical compounding principles only. They are provided for illustrative purposes and should not be interpreted to represent the performance, past or present, of any investment product. Future rates of return cannot be predicted with certainty. None of these illustrations incorporates your personal circumstances or other factors that may be important in making investment decisions.

Saving $150 a month, or just $5 a day, for only 20 years—*and never saving anything else*—is an outlay of $36,000. Yet compounded at an interest rate of 10 percent for 44 years—the length of many people's careers—it would grow to $1.2 million.

Let's imagine instead that when I ask this 21-year-old if he has $1,800, he says no, and that when I ask, "Can you save $150 a month?" he says no and gets tired of me asking questions and leaves. He ends up putting $0 per month away, from age 21 through 41. That comes out to $0 savings for those 20 years.

If you earn 10 percent on $0, when you turn 65 that will have grown to $0!

Pretty easy concept, right? If you save *nothing*, you end up with *nothing*. How about the following concept? If you save *something*, you will end up with *something*. It doesn't take a rocket scientist to work that out, but for you to put it into action, you need to start changing the way you think about money *now*! If your retirement plan is to win the lottery, you will wake up on your 65th birthday realizing that to make ends meet you will have to work forever as a greeter at the local shopping center and eat cat food for supper.

If your retirement plan is to win the lottery, you will have to work forever as a greeter at the local shopping center and eat cat food for supper.

When I am not managing money for my clients, I get to travel and speak to groups about money. Most of the people I speak to are trying to learn about making better financial decisions. Usually half of the audience is young and the other half older. At the end of my presentations, I hear the same things over and over again. The older half always says, "I wish someone had told me to save when I was younger." Some of the younger people say, "Why should I save? I will be dead when I am 65."

I remember when I was 21 years old and had a friend who was 26. I thought he was so old. When you are young, you just think that way. You think that you will live forever and that it is better to have fun with your money instead of putting some of it away for a rainy day. Most people don't start thinking seriously about retirement until they're about 55 years old. Don't wait until you are 55 to start saving. The longer you wait, the more you will have to save. You need to start as soon as possible. Saving has to be a new part of your life—just as when someone wants to get into shape, they have to go to the gym regularly.

Saving has to be a new part of your life—just as when someone wants to get into shape, they have to go to the gym regularly.

PAY YOURSELF FIRST

The most important fact that I want you to take away is that it doesn't take a lot of money to have a lot of money, but it does take for you to start saving now. You need to realize the importance of paying yourself before you pay anybody else—especially if you have little or no money. When I say "pay," I don't want you to confuse that with "give." When you give, you are not doing that out of an obligation—no one is going to cut off your electricity or come repossess your car because you didn't give to

DOLLARS & UNCOMMON SENSE

a worthy cause this month. You give because it helps you learn to spend less, retrains you to think differently about money, and increases the amount of money you have quickly and easily; and because if you give, you will receive. So your overall priorities are still to:

- Give away 10 percent of what you make.
- Save 10 percent (pay yourself).
- Live on the rest.

Who loves you more than anybody else? No, it is not your parents. It is also not the bank, department stores, credit card companies, or utility companies. It is *you*. You love you more than anybody else does, so you should be paying yourself first.

You love you more than anybody else does, so you should be paying yourself first.

Whichever method you use when you pay your utility bills, pay yourself the same way. I don't care if you set up an electronic draft, write yourself a check, or transfer money from your checking to your savings, you need to put yourself on top of the long list of people who get your money. You need to set up an account for *you* and put money into that account before you pay anybody else. The rule is to put at least 10 percent of what you make into that account.

Let's just say that you are still refining your spending plan, and for some reason you cannot pay yourself 10 percent but can only pay yourself 5 percent—what should you do? Do you remember the concept that if you save *nothing*, you end up with *nothing*? I would rather that you save *something* rather than nothing. But keep in mind that for this program to truly have its full benefit, your ultimate goal needs to be to live by the 10-10-80 rule, giving 10 percent, saving 10 percent, and living on the rest.

THE TAKE HOME

- If you save *nothing*, you end up with *nothing*.
- Don't wait till you are 55 to start saving.
- It doesn't take a lot of money to have a lot of money, but it does mean you need to start somewhere and begin saving now.
- Put yourself on top of the long list of people who get your money.
- Set up an account for *you*, and put at least 10 percent of what you make into that account before you pay anybody else.

10: Priorities: "Life Happens," Then "I Quit!"

REVISITING YOUR LIFE HAPPENS ACCOUNT
In Chapter 8, I said that your first priority was to save $1,500 in your Life Happens Account. I do not like to burst your bubble, but that is just a start. Most financial planners recommend that you have enough money in your emergency account to cover at least three to six months' worth of expenses. I have a better recommendation, which will prepare you for the next financial crisis. I call it the 12 by 60 Formula. You will take 60 percent of your monthly income and multiply it by 12, to give you 60 percent of your annual income. That is how much you ultimately need to have saved in your Life Happens Account. Let's say you make $3,000 a month. Sixty percent of $3,000 is $1,800. Multiply that by 12, and you get $21,600, so you would want to have at least $21,600 in your Life Happens Account.

Why so much? My primary goal in this book is to help change the way you think about money, but I also want you to be prepared for the next financial crisis, which will inevitably happen.

During the recent financial crisis, many people either lost their jobs or had their income reduced. Two of my clients come to mind, a husband and wife who are good friends of mine. He had been working in a great job for seven years, and the couple had inherited some money a few years before. They came to me and asked what they should do with their money. I asked them how much they had in their Life Happens Account, and they looked at me like deer in the headlights. I explained that first they should ensure they had enough money in a Life Happens Account to replace 60 percent of their annual income—and then I would make some recommendations for their long-term savings and investments.

I want you to be prepared for the next financial crisis, which will inevitably happen.

Fast-forward about two years: He was laid off from his job and called to thank me for my advice. Though he felt bad and was under a lot of pressure because he'd lost his job, knowing he had a financial cushion to fall back on gave him some relief and, more importantly, time to find another job. Hopefully, you will not lose your job, but you need to always be prepared. Hope for the best and plan for the worst.

Hope for the best and plan for the worst.

The reason I recommend having 60 percent of your annual income in your Life Happens Account is that when things get tough, you can really make some sacrifices and make that 60 percent stretch for a year. Lack of income is a strong motivator to start making drastic cuts, so you should have no problem cutting out 40 percent of your expenses if you lose your job. If your funds last for at least a year, you will have a better probability of finding a job before your money runs out; and then once you find a job, you can start building your savings back up. If you receive some sort of severance package that you can add to your Life Happens Account, you might even be able to stretch things out for 18 months. It is important to ensure you are prepared so that you don't lose everything. I have seen people drain all of their retirement accounts, lose their house, business, family, and even their lives. I cannot stress enough that you need to start thinking differently before it is too late.

Go ahead and multiply your monthly income by 0.60, then multiply that by 12:

_____ x 0.60= _____
(Monthly income)   (60% of monthly income)

_____ x 12= _____
(60% of monthly income)   (Life Happens Account total)

Once you have that number, I don't want you to panic. You are probably thinking that there is no possible way you will ever be able to save that much. I want to share with you the following story. One day I was giving my son a talk about the birds and the bees. From the faces he was making when I was telling him how babies were made, I could see how uncomfortable he was feeling, and I knew exactly what was going on in his head. You see, when I was his age, I was in the same place that he was—and now as an adult I know how good it is. You know what I am talking about, how good sex is. The reason you don't save is that you are thinking just like my child was about the birds and the bees. But I promise, once you start saving, it will feel so good. You will want more and more, and once you reach your goal of having 60 percent of your annual income in your Life Happens Account, you will never be the same. You will never want to go back to how you used to think about savings!

Once you start saving, it will feel so good.

Now that you know how much you need in your Life Happens Account, what type of account should you save that money in? First, your Life Happens Account needs to be in something safe and liquid. No, you are not going to buy water with it. You need to be able to have access to your Life Happens Account at any time, because you never know when you might have an emergency. This means you can't have it in a retirement account, because with a few exceptions, you only have access to a retirement account without penalty only when you turn 59½. It also shouldn't be invested in stocks, real estate, commodities, or any type of financial instrument that can restrict your access to it. I am not telling you that real estate is a bad investment, but if your money is in real estate, how quickly can you get it? Regarding stocks, let's assume you had all of your Life Happens Account in the stock market and the market lost 50 percent of its value—once again, that wouldn't be a good idea.

The money has to be deposited into an account where it can't lose value, which means if you put $1 in, you will get at least $1 out. You just don't want to have it in something you can't get to if "life happens." That would sort of defeat the purpose! The only types of financial instruments you want to consider for your Life Happens Account are FDIC-insured savings accounts, short-term (less than one year) FDIC-insured certificates of deposit (CDs), FDIC-insured money-market accounts, or U.S. Treasury bills.[10] If you do keep some of your Life Happens Account in short-term CDs or U.S. Treasury bills, be sure to also keep at least enough money in other FDIC-insured accounts to live on during their term should you lose your income.

I also want you to consider the interest rate you will be receiving on the money you have deposited. Do not be afraid to shop around for the best rates. Beware of teaser rates. Institutions will give you a great rate up front, but as soon as the introductory time period is up, the rates go way down. They know it is an inconvenience for you to open and close accounts, and they count on that to keep you from shopping around for better rates. If you earn 2 percent on $10,000, that would be $200 of interest; if you earn 1 percent on $10,000, that would be $100 of interest. If I offered you the choice of $200 or $100, which one would you take?

"I QUIT!" ACCOUNT

Money will not buy you long-term happiness, but money will give you choices. For many years, I have had as clients a man who is now 86 and his wife, who is a young 82. They were very good savers and had a lot of money in their retirement accounts. A few years ago, after analyzing their expenses and the income that would be generated from their retirement accounts, I told them they would need to withdraw just 3 percent annually from their account to make ends meet by the time they factored in social

---

10   If held to maturity, U.S. Treasury securities are backed by the full faith and credit of the U.S. government as to the full repayment of principal and interest. But U.S. Treasury securities can fluctuate, and, if sold prior to maturity, may be redeemed for less than their initial investment.

security. The husband looked at me and said that they did not want to pull any money out of their retirement accounts, except what was required of them by the Internal Revenue Service.

Money will not buy you long-term happiness, but money will give you choices.

Assuming that they were a little confused, I tried to explain to them that they would need to pull more money out to cover their expenses. I could see the husband was getting frustrated with me. I asked him if they had other funds they were going to withdraw from. He said no, he was still working, and they didn't need any money from their retirement accounts. I explained to them that he didn't have to work any longer, but it seemed the more I went over the numbers, the more frustrated he became.

For a few years, they would come in, we would go over their accounts, they would tell me they didn't need any money from their retirement savings, and they would go on their way. After a few years, the husband came in for their account review without his wife. I finally asked him, "Why are you working when you don't have to?" He told me he loved his wife, but she gave him too much work when he was at home. He said it was easier for him to put in the hours at work than stay at home having to work on his "honey do" list. He *chose* to work, to keep his sanity and stay happily married.

On the other hand, there is the man I met when I was speaking at a National Guard armory to a unit that was going to be deployed to Afghanistan. After the event, he came up to thank me for my presentation. He looked as though he was at least in his early 60s, so I asked him if he had a family member that was going to be deployed. Family members sometimes attend these events to get information. He told me that he didn't have any family members being deployed, and he was going. He was 63 years old, and this was his third deployment in five years.

I thought about how much he must love his country to volunteer for a third deployment, and how hard it must be in a combat zone in your 60s. What broke my heart came next. He told me that he wished there was someone like me who could have inspired him to start saving earlier. He said he really didn't want to go to Afghanistan, but since he was getting close to retirement age, he needed to start saving. He went on to tell me that the extra money he made from his first two deployments had given him the opportunity to pay off his debts.

As I've said, money won't buy you happiness, but it will give you choices. That 63-year-old did not have any choice. I can understand patriotism being the motivating factor for someone to deploy so many times, but lack of savings should not be the motivating factor for you to put your life on the line.

Do not let time keep slipping by. You need to start putting money away now, before it is too late. Your goal is to have enough money in your "I Quit!" Account so that when you reach retirement age, you have the choice of working or not working.

BALANCING YOUR "LIFE HAPPENS" AND "I QUIT!" PRIORITIES

Right about now you might feel that your head is about to explode trying to work out how to prioritize saving for your Life Happens Account *and* an "I Quit!" Account. But actually, the steps are simple and easy to follow. Each month, when you pay yourself

10 percent of your income, pay it into your savings accounts according to this plan, moving on to the next stage each time you reach a goal:

Table 10-1. How to allocate the 10 percent of income you save each month

STAGE 1	Save 10% into your Life Happens Account.
Goal 1 attained: $1,500 in your Life Happens Account.	
STAGE 2	Save 5% into your Life Happens Account and 5% into your "I Quit!" Account.
Goal 2 attained: 60 percent of annual income in Life Happens Account.	
STAGE 3	Save 10% into your "I Quit!" Account.
Goal 3 attained: "I quit!"	

If you earn $3,000 a month, you will start putting at least $300 a month (10 percent of your monthly income) into your Life Happens Account until it contains $1,500. Once that goal is met, each month you will put half of the $300, which is $150, into your Life Happens Account and the other $150 into your "I Quit!" Account. You will continue to do this until you have 60 percent of your annual income ($21,600) in your Life Happens Account. Once you have met that goal, then you will put the entire $300 into your "I Quit!" Account.

The money in your "I Quit!" Account should be put someplace where it will hopefully grow faster than the money in your Life Happens Account. The next chapter is all about helping you plan the types of savings and investments for your "I Quit!" Account, to ensure that one day you have the option to choose whether to work or not.

THE TAKE HOME

- Save 10 percent of your monthly income into your Life Happens Account until it contains $1,500.
- Then save 5 percent of your monthly income into your Life Happens Account and 5 percent into your "I Quit!" Account.
- Continue doing this each month until your Life Happens Account contains 60 percent of your annual income.
- Once that goal is met, save 10 percent of your monthly income into your "I Quit!" Account.

11: Plan: Invest in Your Future

Your "I Quit!" Account is your investment in your own future. Your aim with that money should therefore be to make a higher return on it compared to what you are getting in your savings or checking account. That means you need to know some basic concepts about investing in assets that have the potential to earn a higher return, such as stocks, bonds, property, and commodities, including oil and gold. It's pretty easy to get bamboozled by the terms you hear advisers using, but believe me, it's not rocket science. You *can* get your head around these concepts. And you *need* to, because by understanding these basic ideas, you will be in a much better position to invest successfully and reach your goal of a fully funded "I Quit!" Account.

I recommend that you sit down with a Certified Financial Planner™ to develop a custom financial plan for you. The purpose of this chapter is to help you understand the concepts and start forming your own ideas for your financial future so that when you walk into your planner's office, you are well-informed and you know where you want to head financially.

And remember, for your investment plan to be successful, you must continue to add at least 10 percent of your income to your investments every month.

RISK

The most fundamental investment concept of all is *risk*. When you invest your money, you have to take a risk to get a higher return than you do when you put your money in a checking or savings account at the bank. Risk equals opportunity. The greater the risk, the greater the potential return, but keep in mind that the greater the risk, the greater the potential loss. You should never invest money that you are not willing to lose. I don't care whether you're investing in a house, a property, stocks, bonds, gold, or any other investment: You can lose your money. Later in the chapter, we'll talk about how to choose the level of risk that you are personally comfortable with so that you can plan your investment strategy, but before you are ready for that, you need to know a few other basic concepts about investing.

ASSET ALLOCATION

Asset allocation is how you divide your money among different classes of assets—that is, what percentages of your money are in cash, bonds, stocks, and alternative investments, such as real estate or commodities.[11] When you combine the different classes of assets, you do so to obtain the most return for a given level of

---

11   Asset allocation does not ensure or guarantee better performance and cannot eliminate the risk of investment losses.

risk, or the least risk for a given level of return. The way you have your assets allocated is the decision that has the greatest impact on your investment return.[12]

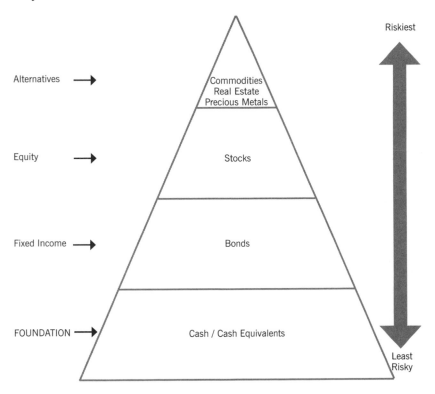

It is helpful to think of asset allocation like spreading your money throughout the levels of a pyramid, with the least risky asset classes at the bottom, tapering up to the most risky

---

12   Brinson, Hood, and Beebower, "Determinants of Portfolio Performance," *Financial Analysts Journal*, July–August 1986, found that more than 90 percent of a portfolio's performance results from allocation across asset classes.

asset classes at the top. I want to point out that there is no such thing as one correct way to allocate your assets, because different types of assets have different levels of risk and return; and because people have different goals and different tolerance for risk, and are at different stages in their lives. For instance, the way a 25-year-old who might have a high tolerance for risk and may not need the money for a long time allocates assets might differ from the way a 64-year-old who is planning to retire soon and has a more conservative approach invests.

At the bottom level of the pyramid, you have your foundation, which is *cash*. Your foundation could be your savings accounts or may be certificates of deposit (CDs). You will not get a high rate of return on cash, but you also do not want to make your foundation risky. It has to be solid. You wouldn't knowingly build your house on a weak foundation. A strong foundation would be a fully funded Life Happens Account.

You wouldn't knowingly build your house on a weak foundation.

Next is the *fixed-income level*, or *bonds*. How bonds work is that you loan your money to a company or government for a specified period of time, and in return they give you interest payments. This type of investing is riskier than the cash level, so you have the opportunity to get a higher return on your money. For the added risk, you have the opportunity to earn more money.

The next level up the pyramid is *equity*, or ownership of a company. When you buy *stocks*, also known as *shares*, in a company, you become a partial owner. As an owner, you are entitled to a portion of the profits of the company, which are paid in the form of *dividends*. You could also be rewarded if the company grows and its stock price increases.

The top level of the pyramid is *alternatives*. Some examples are investments in commodities—such as oil, natural gas, and precious metals—or hard assets, such as real estate. Alternatives are usually the riskiest investments, because their prices tend to rise and fall with greater volatility.

DIVERSIFICATION

Diversification means spreading your money among different investments within one asset class. Diversification does not eliminate risk or protect you from losing money, but it does help you avoid unsystematic risk. *Systematic risk* affects an entire market— an example is when prices plunge across the board on news of a change in interest rates, a recession, or a war. *Unsystematic risk* affects just one stock or a handful of stocks. If you have all of your eggs in one basket—that is, you have all of your money in one stock or one investment—you are more exposed to unsystematic risk and can lose a lot of money very fast. Simply put, you do not want to put all your eggs in one basket. A good example of why not is Lehman Brothers. If you had all of your money in Lehman Brothers stock on Friday, September 12, 2008, when you woke up on Monday morning, September 15, 2008, all of your money would have been lost.

I lost some money that way myself, because I allowed greed to get the best of me. I am always telling my clients to be diversified, and for some reason I did not take my own advice. I fell into the trap I always warn my clients of: I allowed my emotions to override my better judgment. A few weeks prior, an investment bank was bailed out, and its stock price shot straight up. I thought that Lehman Brothers was going to be bailed out or at least that some other financial entity would purchase them, and the stock price would shoot up. At the same time, I was also considering buying another investment-banking stock on which I thought I could make some real quick money.

I fell into the trap I always warn my clients of: I allowed my emotions to override my better judgment.

I had $3,000 to invest, and on Friday, September 12, 2008, I spent it all on Lehman Brothers stock. On the night of Sunday, September 14, 2008, as I was surfing the internet, Lehman Brothers announced they would be closing their doors. The stock I had invested in on Friday was now worthless. If I had invested half of the money in Lehman Brothers and half in the other investment-banking stock I was considering, at least I wouldn't have lost all of the $3,000 I had invested that Friday.

I want to share with you the story of one of my clients who would have lost a lot more than $3,000 if he didn't follow my advice. My office is in Charlotte, North Carolina. Before the credit crisis hit, most people were unaware that Charlotte is one of the largest financial districts outside of New York City. Around the beginning of the year in 2007, a senior vice president from Wachovia came in for an appointment to review his assets. He had been referred to me by one of my existing clients. During our initial appointment, I conducted an inventory of his assets and asked him a whole bunch of questions, which I pored over after he left. He had $2.1 million in his 401(k), and more than $1.8 million, or almost 90 percent, of that was in Wachovia stock. The rest of it was in large-cap mutual funds and cash. Here was someone who worked in the banking industry, yet he had almost all of his eggs in one basket. It raised a red flag for me.

A few weeks later, he came back in to hear my recommendations. The first thing I told him was that I would never recommend that anyone have more than 20 percent of their assets in one stock. I remember seeing his eyebrows rising. Before I could get another word out of my mouth, he informed me that he had worked in the banking industry for more than 30 years and had accumulated all of his wealth from his company stock, and that the only reason I was telling him to diversify was so I could make more money by selling his stock and investing his money somewhere else. He was clearly upset.

I took a deep breath to gather my composure and told him that because I am paid on a percentage of the assets I manage (1 percent), I would get paid the same amount whether all his money was in Wachovia stock or not. I told him that I would make more money when his account went up and less money when his account went down. At the end of the day, I work so I can feed my family, so even if I didn't care about him or his retirement account, it was in my own best interest to give him the best advice, because I do care about me. I told him that my best interest was his best interest.

There was a long, awkward silence. I told him I understood that he was able to accumulate all of his wealth because of the company he worked for, so there were emotions involved. And then I asked him, "Do you remember the commercials a long time ago about E. F. Hutton?" The slogan went "When E. F. Hutton speaks, people listen." When I said that, I saw his demeanor change, and the wheels started spinning in his mind. He remembered that when he first got into the banking industry, E. F. Hutton was the second-largest brokerage firm in the United States. He also remembered that weeks before the crash of 1987, E. F. Hutton came extremely close to collapsing, and would have if it hadn't been for a merger that took effect in 1988. Imagine a company that had survived the Great Depression almost going broke.

> *Imagine having $1.8 million of Wachovia stock in your retirement account, and then one day you look at your statement and see you have only around $190,000 left.*

In early January of 2007, my client's Wachovia stock was valued at around $56 a share. By December of 2008, Wachovia stock was trading at around $5.54 a share. The stock dropped by more than 90 percent. Imagine having $1.8 million of Wachovia stock in your retirement account, and then one day you look at your statement and see you have only around $190,000 left. Fortunately, that did not happen to my client, because he had taken my advice and diversified.

Diversification of Equities

Equities are classified according to company size. You can invest in *small companies*, *midsize companies*, and *large companies*. Shares in small companies are known as small-capitalization, or small-cap, stocks. Shares in large companies are known as large-capitalization, or large-cap, stocks. Midsize are somewhere in the middle and are called mid caps. Something to know is that smaller companies can grow quickly and bring a faster return on one's investment, but small-capitalization stocks have an increased risk of price fluctuations. Small-capitalization stocks that have above-average earnings may be more volatile, especially if earnings do not continue to grow. Small-capitalization companies tend to be more volatile than the stock market as a whole. They have fewer resources at their disposal and can go out of business more easily than larger companies. That is why it's smart to diversify so that you have some of your money in small companies, some in mid-size companies, and some in large companies.

Another way to diversify is by investing in not only U.S. stocks but also *international equities*. International investing involves special risks, because of specific factors such as increased volatility, currency fluctuations, economic instability, political developments, and differences in auditing and other financial standards. But the next Google could be Chinese, German, or even Australian. There are many great companies that are outside of the United States, so it could be a good idea to have some of your money there also.

Diversification of Bonds

When it comes to bond diversification, there are several things to be mindful of: *quality*, *time*, and *interest-rate risk*. *Quality* refers to the dependability of the company you are loaning your money to and the probability of getting your money back. For example, if you lend your money to the government by buying a Treasury bond, the chances are good that you will get your money back. Treasury bonds are not subject to credit risk (the risk that you won't get your money back) if held to maturity, because they are guaranteed by the full faith and credit of the U.S. government. Be aware, though, that if these securities are sold prior to maturity, the investor may receive less than the original amount invested. Since you are loaning your money to the government when you buy a treasury bond, the risk is low; and in turn, the return will be low.[13] On the other hand, if you loan your money to a company, you expect to get a higher rate of return on your investment, since that company is not as big as the government and cannot print money to pay you back.

How accurately can you predict the probability of a company going bankrupt in one year, five years, or 10 years?

Time, also referred to in the finance industry as *duration*, refers to how long you are going to let someone borrow your money. Usually, the shorter the time, the lower the rate you will receive; and the longer the time, the higher the rate. That is because the longer the time, the more risk you are usually assuming. How accurately can you predict the probability of a company going bankrupt in one year, five years, or 10 years? You might be able to look out a year or so, but it is extremely hard to predict what type of financial condition a company will be in 10 years from now.

If in 2000 you bought a five-year company bond, you would have been paid interest throughout those five years and would have had your principal (your initial investment) returned at maturity, in 2005. Let's say that instead, in 2000 you purchased a 10-year bond in that company, and in June 2008 it went out of business. You would have been paid interest up to June 2008, but since the company went out of business, you would not get your principal back.

---

13   Investing in bonds is subject to certain risks, including interest-rate risk and inflation risk. As interest rates rise, the prices of bonds fall. Long-term bonds are more exposed to interest-rate risk than short-term bonds.

To sum up, the longer the time until the bond matures, the more risk you will assume. Just because a company is doing well now, that does not guarantee it will be doing well 10 years from now. You have the opportunity to earn a higher return for taking the added risk.

The longer the time until the bond matures, the more risk you will assume.

Another risk you have to consider with bonds is *interest-rate risk*. To understand this idea, think of bond prices and interest rates as a teeter-totter.

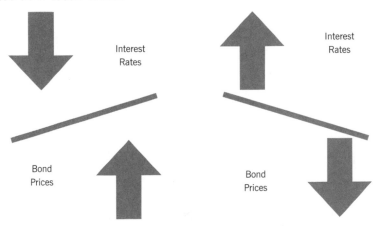

Figure 11-2. When interest rates go down, bond prices go up, and vice versa.

When interest rates go down, bond prices go up; and when interest rates go up, bond prices go down. If you own a bunch of long-term bonds and interest rates go up, you could lose money if you cash them in prior to maturity, since when interest rates go up, bond prices go down. A strategy to consider when you diversify the bond, or fixed-income, level of your investment pyramid is to have some of it allocated in short-term bonds, some in intermediate, and some in long-term bonds. You also want to consider having some of your bonds in government or other higher-quality bonds and some in lower-quality bonds.

Individual bonds can present greater opportunities for income, but because they are not diversified portfolios of securities, you will be exposed to a higher degree of credit risk. So before purchasing any individual bond, or any other undiversified investment, please seek out the advice of a qualified professional adviser.

Diversification of Alternatives

To diversify in this asset level of the investment pyramid, you can invest your money in a mix of oil, natural gas, gold, silver, and real estate to name a few. Alternative investments carry more risk than other asset classes. For instance, investing in real estate subjects an investor to risks including possible declines in the value of real estate, risks related to economic conditions, possible lack of availability of mortgage funds, overbuilding, and extended vacancies of properties. Investing in oil has its risks, also. When oil prices are booming, everybody wants to get in on the action, but will the price of oil remain high or eventually go lower? If the economy takes a downturn, oil demand will probably decrease, and therefore the price of oil will go down. The same goes for precious metals. They are *very* volatile, speculative, and high-risk investments.

I am not recommending that you should or should not put money into these types of investments. What I am recommending is that if you are considering making them a part of your investment plan, you sit down with a knowledgeable professional who can explain the good and the bad so you can make your own judgment.

WHAT KIND OF INVESTOR ARE YOU?

There are three types of investor. The first is the *conservative* investor. This person does not want to assume any risk, or only minimal risk. Conservative investors have to accept lower investment returns for taking lower risk. There is nothing wrong with that. Conservative investors would have their money in cash and bonds.

A *balanced* investor is someone who assumes somewhat more risk than a conservative investor, in exchange for the potential of higher returns. This added risk also means a greater potential for loss. This type of investor owns a balanced mix of stocks and bonds. Keep in mind that in the long term, stocks have outperformed bonds and other fixed-income investments, but that's not a guarantee.

An *aggressive* investor assumes the most risk. For assuming the highest risk, aggressive investors have the potential to earn the highest returns. They also have the potential to lose the most money. Aggressive investors usually have a higher percentage of money in stocks than conservative and balanced investors do. Aggressive investors have a lower percentage of money in bonds, or in order to yield higher returns, they invest in bonds that are considered lower quality (that is, riskier). They may also have some alternative investments in the mix.

Your personal investment plan depends upon how much risk you are willing to take. The funny thing is, most people don't have a very accurate perception of what kind of investor they are. Let me give you an analogy. If I hear an animal making a quacking noise, and I see that it has an orange beak and orange webbed feet, I can tell you that animal is a duck. Now, there is nothing wrong with a duck. But there is something wrong if that duck says it is an eagle.

Most people when they invest their money think they are something they are not. That is why most people are not successful when they invest their money. For example, they say they want to take more risk, but when the markets go down, they panic and sell their investments at lower prices than what they paid for them. They thought they were eagles, but they went quack quack.

I am going to help you figure out what type of animal you are. The first thing I want you to do is go to a website. I am reluctant to share too many secrets, but since you purchased the book, I will go ahead and give you the address of this pretty important website. Go to your computer and type this in: w – w – w – g – o – o – g – l – e.

You are probably thinking to yourself, "What a smart-ass." The truth is, there are a bunch of financial planning tools available on the internet, and they are as close as a Google search away. These tools can be very helpful, so long as you don't forget to consult with a Certified Financial Planner™ before you make any financial decisions.

For now, I want you to Google "investment risk tolerance." If you do that, the first few results should be resources that can help you assess your own risk tolerance.

One of the links that comes up should lead you to the Rutgers University website, where you will find an investment risk tolerance quiz (http://njaes.rutgers.edu/money/riskquiz). I should point out that I don't have any association with the folks at Rutgers; I just think that their risk quiz is a great way to find out where you lie on the scale of conservative to aggressive investor. You will be asked a series of questions that gauge how tolerant you are of taking risks when investing. It is important that you answer the questions honestly. If you are a duck, you want to answer like a duck, not an eagle, and vice versa. If you do not answer the questions honestly, it will do you no good. You will be asked multiple-choice questions about your age, income, financial responsibilities, job security, financial know-how, and attitudes toward money and risk. You will also have some interesting multiple-choice hypotheticals posed to you, such as what you would do if you lost your job just before you were about to leave for an expensive vacation, and what you would do if you unexpectedly received $20,000 to invest.

Once you have answered all of the questions, click next, and your results will be displayed. Depending on your score, your tolerance for risk will be ranked as high, above average, average/moderate, below average, or low.

The quiz should take you less than 15 minutes to complete. It will be 15 minutes well spent, because the results will give you an idea of how you should allocate and diversify your investments to suit your risk tolerance. If you are a duck and answered the questions like a duck, or you are an eagle and answered the questions like an eagle, this is a great tool that can help you decide on how much risk you should take. You can show the results to your

If you are more conservative, you will have to save a lot more than someone who is not as conservative.

Certified Financial Planner™, as they will help you both arrive at an investment plan suited to your personality and circumstances.

Whatever type of investor you are, you can reach your financial goal. Keep in mind, though, that if you are more conservative, you will have to save a lot more than someone who is not as conservative. Table 11-1 is a hypothetical example showing what it would take to have $500,000 at the age of 65, depending on the age at which an investor began saving and the hypothetical compounding rate the investments earned. For example, at a hypothetical 7 percent compounding rate, a 30-year-old today who wants to retire at age 65 with $500,000 would need to save at least $278 per month to reach that goal.

Table 11-1. Hypothetical example of monthly savings required to have $500,000 by age 65

	3%	5%	7%	9%	11%	Compound Rate
20	$438	$247	$132	$68	$33	
25	$540	$328	$190	$107	$58	
30	$674	$440	$278	$170	$101	
35	$858	$601	$410	$273	$178	
40	$1,121	$840	$617	$446	$317	
45	$1,523	$1,216	$960	$749	$578	

Starting Age

It is important to remember that all scenarios are hypothetical examples of mathematical compounding principles only. They are provided for illustrative purposes and should not be interpreted to represent the performance, past or present, of any investment product. Future rates of return cannot be predicted with certainty. None of these illustrations incorporates your personal circumstances or other factors that may be important in making investment decisions.

KEEP EMOTIONS OUT OF INVESTING

Whether you are a conservative, balanced, or aggressive investor, do not allow your emotions to influence your investment strategy. One of the key traits of my clients who have money is that they do not allow their emotions to influence their financial decisions.

The uncommon sense approach to investing is to buy low and sell high. You are probably thinking that it is *common* sense to buy low and sell high. But if it was common mon sense, when the markets went down, people would buy; and when the markets went up, people would sell. That almost *never* happens. Most investors assume more risk when markets are up and take fewer risks when markets are down. That's because most investors are emotional investors who don't have their eye on the long-term result. That can be potentially costly. If you jump in and out of the markets based on whether they are up or down, you run the risk of missing out on the markets' powerful rallies. You get caught off guard.

The uncommon sense approach to investing is to buy low and sell high. That almost never happens.

History has shown that the average annual rate of return on investments becomes less variable over time. That's because if you watch the markets daily, they go up and down, but if you look at them over a longer period of time, such as years or decades, the trend lines for the markets go up. On a daily basis, the markets can rise and fall in a volatile way; but over a period of 20 years, the peaks and valleys smooth out.

In Figure 11.3, the graph on the left charts the closing price of the Standard & Poor's (S&P 500) stock market index each day from January 3, 2011, through June 1, 2011, and it shows a lot of variability. The graph on the right also charts the S&P 500's closing prices during the same period, but on a monthly basis instead of daily, and it shows much less variability.

Figure 11-3. On a daily basis, markets go up and down; but they trend upward over time.

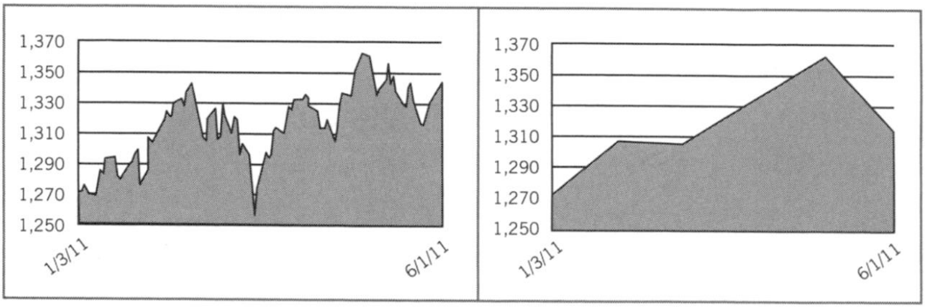

S&P 500 Daily Closing Prices, Jan.–June 2011   S&P 500 Monthly Closing Prices, Jan.–June 2011

Past performance is no guarantee of future results. These graphs are for illustration purposes only and not indicative of any investment. The Standard & Poor's 500 (S&P 500) is an unmanaged group of securities considered to be representative of the stock market in general. An investment cannot be made directly in an index.

Because in the long term markets have a tendency to go up, you should not let the short-term ups and downs affect your emotions and, more importantly, your investment decisions. The stock market, real estate market, commodities market, and so on can offer many great opportunities for the long-term investor, but they can be devastating for those who buy and sell in the short term.

Your investment starts off as a small acorn, and it takes many years to become an oak tree.

Most people think a long time is a month, but when it comes to investing, you have to think in years. Think of your investment like an oak tree. It starts off as a small acorn, and it takes many years to become an oak tree.

There are no safe and reliable shortcuts when it comes to investing. Do you really believe that if someone had a shortcut they would sell it to you in a newsletter on the internet? Those people use your emotions—greed and fear—to get you to pay for their great secret or magical formula, which only succeeds in making them richer and you poorer.

Many investors become more aggressive when markets are doing well and move their money into riskier types of investments; and then when markets are doing poorly, they become more conservative, selling their riskier investments to purchase less risky and less volatile ones. During the summer of 2008, oil was at $145 a barrel, and there were analysts saying that it could go to $250 a barrel. A few of my conservative investors wanted to move some of their money into oil. I advised them against doing that, explaining to them that oil is a commodity and commodities in general are extremely risky. A few months later, oil was at $32 a barrel.

When markets are not doing well, in the short term you see your investments losing more and more value, and your emotions try to convince you to protect what you have by selling those investments. I see the same mistake time and time again: When the markets go down by 10 percent, people have the tendency to panic and move their money from riskier assets, such as stocks, to less risky asset classes, such as cash.

Buying low and selling high works in good markets and in bad markets. Selling low and buying high never works.

Regardless of whether you are a conservative, balanced, or aggressive investor, you should not allow the direction of the markets or your emotions to change your risk level. Buying low and selling high works in good markets and in bad markets. Selling low and buying high never works.

I want you to think of it like this: If you move your money into safer investments when the markets dip, in the short term you might avoid a possible 15 percent loss. That's good, right? Not if that means you are missing out on a possible gain of 25 percent in the long term. Financially, you would actually be ahead if you lost 15 percent now but later gained 25 percent. But guess what? Our minds are not wired that way. What do you think most people would do if they had a rough day and were offered the choice of a free 15-minute massage now or a free 25-minute massage 72 hours from now? You guessed it: Most people would take the 15-minute massage now instead of waiting, even though a 25-minute massage 72 hours later is worth a lot more.

The same concept applies to investing. Your emotions process that it would feel better to not lose 15 percent now than it would to gain 25 percent later. When you lose money, you actually feel pain. If you put your hand on a hot stove, you automatically remove your hand from the source of pain. If you lose money, you instinctively want to move your money into conservative choices to get away from the source of the pain. Doing so can end up costing you in a way that will take you a very long time to recover from.

When you lose money, you actually feel pain.

Let's say an investor had a sound investment plan. This investor had $10,000 in quality stocks and bonds, and they were properly diversified. Then the markets fell, and the investments lost 50 percent of their value, or $5,000. This investor will have to get a 100 percent return just to recoup that loss. That's because it will take $5,000 to get back to $10,000, and $5,000 is 100 percent of the remaining $5,000.

If this investor panicked and sold the investments, and put that $5,000 into a CD that paid 3 percent interest, it would take roughly 24 years to make up that loss. This calculation is based on the Rule of 72, a tool commonly used in finance to work out how many years it will take to double a sum of money at a certain interest rate. You simply divide 72 by the interest rate. As 72 ÷ 3 = 24, it will take this investor 24 years to double $5,000 in a CD earning 3 percent interest. On the other hand, if this person left the $5,000 in the original investments and those investments were able to earn 7 percent every year, it would take only 10 years to double in value (72 ÷ 7 = 10.2).

What I recommend is to stay invested and not panic. There are no guarantees, but I think the market would come back sooner than in 24 years, don't you?

You could jump in and out of the markets if you had a Magic 8 Ball that told you when the markets were about to fall and you should sell, and when they had hit bottom and you better buy. Unfortunately, there isn't a Magic 8 Ball that can do that. It is nearly impossible to time things perfectly. Just as lightning doesn't strike the same place twice, you won't get out at the top and then get back in at the bottom.

Some financial pundits try to predict the future, but I seriously doubt anyone who says they know for certain the direction the markets will take in the short term. It's a 50-50 probability on any given day. The odds improve as the time horizon gets longer. What I am telling you applies not only to good markets but also to bad markets. You have to keep focused on your long-term goals.

Reason dictates that when you have come up with an investment plan that is grounded in logic, you shouldn't start making changes to it based upon your emotional response to movements in the markets. Your chances of success will be much greater if you listen to the logical side of your brain. So once you have come up with an investment plan, you need to stick with it. The easiest way to get over the temptation to buy and sell short term is to not

Once you have come up with an investment plan, you need to stick with it.

watch the markets minute by minute, hour by hour, day by day. When you are tempted to overreact, meet with your adviser and review your investment plan. What you don't want to do is panic and cash out.

Don't allow the current news or the value of your most recent investment statement to scare you into doing something that will feel good in the short term but in the long term you may not recover from. Remember that the emotions of the moment always distract you from your purpose. You have to possess the courage to stay focused, remain on course, and not let the emotional roller coaster get the best of you. Historically, individuals have turned tail at exactly the wrong time, so there's wisdom in sticking with your plan.

The past should remind you that we have always had crises and market turmoil to overcome. Emotions drive your behavior, and others will try to take advantage of that. It becomes really problematic if your fear causes you to act irrationally, and a negative feedback loop is created, which is very hard to break. It works like this: Once the markets begin to fall, some investors may expect the markets to fall further, and they refrain from buying, even though it would make sense to buy at a lower price, because they think a better bargain might be available tomorrow. Instead, the investors sell when it might logically be a better time to buy.

You must remind yourself that you can neither predict nor control the inherent risks in any of the markets. Instead, you can deal with that risk with a sound investment strategy, which includes proper asset allocation, diversification, and patience. It is *time* and not *timing* that leads to investment rewards. Normally the only time you can get hurt while riding a roller coaster is when you get off it while it is still moving.

Normally the only time you can get hurt while riding a roller coaster is when you get off it while it is still moving.

As a final reminder, the "buy low, sell high" philosophy is always a better strategy in all kinds or markets, no matter if you are a conservative, balanced, or aggressive investor. What will not work is if you add more risk when the markets are doing well or if you decrease risk when the markets are doing poorly. When you do that, you are actually buying high and selling low. Do not change the type of investor you are according to the direction of the markets; and don't risk more then you are willing to lose, no matter what return you think you can get.

WHEN CAN YOU QUIT?

So how much money do you need to save before you can say "I Quit!"?

The following information is a guide and will hopefully get you close. There are many calculators on the web and many books that say you need to have a particular amount, but I believe that rather than setting a fixed amount, you should calculate how much you need for retirement based on what you currently spend. This is another reason why it is so important for you to assess your spending and have a Spending Plan: Unless you know how much you will be spending, you will have no idea how much you need for retirement.

To calculate how much money you need to save in your "I Quit!" Account, do the following three steps.

Step 1:

Calculate your annual income needs.

Multiply your monthly income by 0.60, and multiply the result by 12.

Example: $3,000 × 0.60 = $1,800

$1,800 × 12 = $21,600

Step 2:

Calculate your *before-inflation* "I Quit!" number.

Divide your annual income needs by 0.05.

Example: $21,600 ÷ 0.05 = $432,000

Step 3:

Calculate your *after-inflation* "I Quit!" number.

If you want to quit in 10 years, multiply your before-inflation number by 1.25

15 years, multiply your before-inflation number by 1.50

20 years, multiply your before-inflation number by 1.75

25 years, multiply your before-inflation number by 2

30 years, multiply your before-inflation number by 2.25

35 years, multiply your before-inflation number by 2.50

40 years, multiply your before-inflation number by 2.75

Example: If you want to retire in 20 years, the calculation is $432,000 × 1.75 = $756,000. So in order to quit in 20 years, you will need to build your "I Quit!" Account up to $756,000 in that period of time. If you want to retire in 30 years, the calculation is $432,000 × 2.25 = $972,000.

The number you come up with will be scary. I would like to say you will be able to count on Social Security to make up some of your shortfall, but I would not want you to count on that. It is much safer for you to prepare for the worst and hope for the best.

I want to leave you with some hypothetical examples of how it *is* possible to build the wealth you need to be in a position to say "I Quit!"

If a 25-year-old can save about $1,000 a year, or $82 a month, or quit wasting $2.70 a day, for 30 years, using mathematical compounding at 10 percent, that money would grow to $500,000 by age 65.

Table 11-2a. Hypothetical result of saving $1,000 per year for 30 years

Daily Savings	$2.70
Monthly Savings	$82.00
Annual Savings	$984.00
Years Saved	30 (age starting 25, age ending 55)
Months Saved	360
Interest Rate	10.00%
Future Value	$185,360.01
Years of Growth	10 (to age 65)
FUTURE VALUE	**$501,777.24**

It is important to remember that all scenarios are hypothetical examples of mathematical compounding principles only. They are provided for illustrative purposes and should not be interpreted to represent the performance, past or present, of any investment product. Future rates of return cannot be predicted with certainty. None of these illustrations incorporates your personal circumstances or other factors that may be important in making investment decisions.

If this 25-year-old can save nothing for the year, which comes to saving nothing for the month, and continues wasting $2.70 every day for the next 30 years, and can earn 10 percent on that nothing, I promise you that at age 65 this person will have *nothing*!

Table 11-2b. If you save nothing, you end up with nothing

Daily Savings	$0.00
Monthly Savings	$0.00
Annual Savings	$0.00
Years Saved	30 (age starting 25, age ending 55)
Months Saved	360
Interest Rate	10.00%
Future Value	$0.00
Years of Growth	10 (to age 65)
FUTURE VALUE	**$0.00**

I have another hypothetical example, using a 35-year-old who can save about $2,658 a year, or $222 a month, or quit wasting $7.28 a day, for 30 years. Using mathematical compounding at 10 percent, that money could grow to $500,000.

Table 11-3. Hypothetical result of saving $2,658 per year for 30 years

Daily Savings	$7.28
Monthly Savings	$221.50
Annual Savings	$2,658.00
Years Saved	30 (age starting 35, age ending 65)
Months Saved	360

Interest Rate	10.00%
Future Value	$500,698.08
Years of Growth	0 (to age 65)
FUTURE VALUE	**$500,698.08**

It is important to remember that all scenarios are hypothetical examples of mathematical compounding principles only. They are provided for illustrative purposes and should not be interpreted to represent the performance, past or present, of any investment product. Future rates of return cannot be predicted with certainty. None of these illustrations incorporates your personal circumstances or other factors that may be important in making investment decisions.

Let's say, though, that this 35-year-old can save nothing for the year, which comes to saving nothing for the month, and continues wasting $7.28 every day for the next 30 years, and can earn 10 percent on that nothing. I promise you that this person will have nothing! Are you getting the point?

YOUR FINANCIAL FUTURE

Now it is up to you to start thinking differently about your money. The power to change your financial future is in your hands.

You might feel overwhelmed when you see how much you need in your "I Quit!" Account. You might think, "I will never be able to come up with that much money. I will never be able to quit!" But let me tell you, if you change your spending habits, take control of your debt, and stick to a sound saving and investment plan, your financial future will look far different from what you can imagine right now. Remember, most of my clients are not doctors, lawyers, or corporate executives. They are everyday people just like you who have worked hard, lived within their means, and put a little money away each month.

I was right there in the same shoes you are probably in. I had nothing in my savings, I had a ton of credit card debt, and I couldn't even spell *retirement*. But once I started to change the way I thought, I started spending less. I was able to put money into my savings and pay off that credit card debt, and now I have a decent amount in my retirement account. It didn't happen overnight, but it did happen. I have no doubt that if I can do it, you can, too!

THE TAKE HOME

- The greater the risk of an investment, the greater the potential return; and the greater the risk, the greater the potential loss.
- In order of least risky to most risky, the four major asset classes are cash, bonds, equities (stocks), and alternative investments (commodities).
- Asset allocation (how you divide your money among different classes of assets) has the greatest impact on your investment return.
- Diversification (having a mix of investments within an asset class) does not eliminate risk, but it does help avoid the risk associated with having all your eggs in one basket.
- Determine whether you are a conservative, balanced, or aggressive investor by doing an investment risk tolerance quiz online, and plan your investing accordingly.

- Whatever type of investor you are, you can reach your financial goal, but the more conservative you are, the more you should plan on saving.
- In the long term, markets trend upward, so do not let the short-term ups and downs affect your emotions and your investment decisions.
- You can neither predict nor control the inherent risks in any of the markets. Instead, deal with that risk with a sound investment strategy, which includes proper asset allocation, diversification, and patience.
- Once you have come up with an investment plan, stick with it.

Useful Websites[14]

AnnualCreditReport.com
www.annualcreditreport.com

Here you can request to get your free annual credit report from the three nationwide consumer credit reporting companies: Equifax, Experian, and TransUnion. In January, I order my credit report from Equifax; in May, I order one from Experian; and in September, I order one from TransUnion.

Bankrate.com
www.bankrate.com

This is a good site to compare the banks' interest rates for everything from savings accounts to mortgages. Always take the time to shop around for the best deal.

---

14   Each user who accesses these links, whether directly or indirectly, agrees to the following terms and conditions: These links have been provided solely as a convenience to the reader. Each of these websites is operated or maintained by an entity other than the author. Furthermore, the author is not affiliated with the owners or operators of these websites. Consequently, the author has no control over the content and makes no representations, warranties, or assurances as to the accuracy, currency, or completeness of the information provided on any of these websites. As a reminder, a qualified financial adviser should be consulted prior to making any investment decision. Consequently, it is the reader's responsibility to independently verify any information which may appear on these websites. The author disclaims, without limitation, all liability for any loss or damage of any kind, including any direct or consequential damages, which might be incurred through the use of, or access to, any mentioned websites or to any links to third-party websites. None of the information that is published or referenced constitutes a solicitation, offer, recommendation, or consideration to conclude any legal act. All information is subject to change, or correction without notice. Some links may lead to third-party websites, which are completely outside of the author's control. As a result, the author does not assume any responsibility for the accuracy, completeness, or legality of the contents of these, or any other third-party websites.

Better Business Bureau
www.bbb.org
I tell prospective new clients that people do business with people whom they like and trust. This site is a great resource for checking on a business to see if they have had any customer complaints.

Certified Financial Planner Board of Standards, Inc.
www.cfp.net
Not only can you use this site to find a Certified Financial Planner™, but you can use this site to find out how you can become one also!

Choose to Save
www.choosetosave.org/ballpark
This site provides an easy-to-use two-page worksheet that can help you estimate how much you will need to save for a comfortable retirement.

Consumer Reports
www.consumerreports.org/cro/cars/used-cars/index.htm
This site has guides to used-car buying and other helpful resources. It should be the first place you go to start doing research before you go car shopping.

Crestmont Research
www.crestmontresearch.com/stock-market
This site has great information about the stock market. It has very good visuals and easy-to-understand information.

Federal Reserve
www.federalreserve.gov
At the Federal Reserve's site, you can get a lot of information with regards to the economy and banking. You can also go there to check out rates on certain financial instruments.

Yahoo! Finance
www.finance.yahoo.com
This is a good place to read information regarding the stock market. From its articles to its commentary, this is a website worth checking out.

FloodSmart.gov
www.floodsmart.gov
On the right-hand side of this site's homepage, there is a red box where you can complete a one-step risk profile to determine whether you need flood insurance. A misconception is that homeowner's insurance covers floods.

Google
www.google.com
Seriously, I really like using this search engine to find financial information quickly!

Insurance Information Institute
www.iii.org
This is a great site where you can learn about most types of insurance. This should be one of the first sites you go to if you are considering any type of insurance.

MortgageHelpNow.org
www.mortgagehelpnow.org

This link, which is part of the National Foundation for Credit Counseling's website, has information that can help you if you are considering buying a home, or you need counseling on foreclosure prevention or other types of mortgage counseling.

National Bureau of Economic Research
www.nber.org

This site has a lot of helpful information regarding the economy. Some of it is heavy reading, but you can really learn a lot about what is going on in the economy now and what has happened in the past.

National Foundation for Credit Counseling
www.nfcc.org

The National Foundation for Credit Counseling is the country's largest financial counseling organization and provides links to help regarding credit counseling, housing counseling, bankruptcy counseling and education, and other financial issues.

PowerPay
www.powerpay.org

This is a great website where you can put together a customized get-out-of-debt plan. You can also use this website to develop a budget/spending plan.

Savingforcollege.com
www.savingforcollege.com

This site has a simple calculator you can use to estimate what it will cost to go to college. You can also get good information regarding the different routes to choose from when you are planning for college.

Sileo on Identity Theft, Business Success, Social Media
www.sileo.com

Identity theft is a growing problem that can impact your financial health. You can visit this site to get tools and tips for bulletproofing yourself against identity theft, from one of the the top identity-theft experts, John Sileo.

Repak Financial Services
www.repakfs.com

Yes, this is my site. As my friend Scott Woller, who is a chief master sergeant in the Air Force, would say, "Shameless self-promotion." Seriously, though, you can use my site to find useful information, including financial calculators and other resources.

TreasuryDirect
www.treasurydirect.gov/indiv/tools/tools_savingsbondwizard.htm

I use this website to calculate the value of savings bonds, but you can also use it to get information about the different types of savings bonds and download a calculator to work out the value of any bonds you have.

Glossary

12 by 60 Formula: A formula in which you take 60 percent of your monthly salary and multiply it by 12. This figure is the amount you need to save into your Life Happens Account, and it forms the basis for calculating how much you need in your "I Quit!" Account.

aggressive investor: An investor who assumes the most risk and therefore has the potential to earn the highest return or lose the most money. Compared to other investors, an aggressive investor usually has a higher percentage of money in stocks; has a lower percentage in bonds or has lower-quality bonds; and may have some alternative investments.

alternative investments: Investments in commodities—such as oil, natural gas, and precious metals—or hard assets, such as real estate. Alternative investments are usually the riskiest, because their prices tend to rise and fall with greater volatility than the prices of other investments.

asset allocation: The way your money is divided among different classes of assets—that is, the percentages of your money that are in cash, bonds, stocks, and alternative investments.

balanced investor: An investor who balances risk and return by owning a balanced mix of stocks and bonds. A balanced investor assumes more risk than a conservative investor and less than an aggressive one.

bond: An investment in which an investor loans money to a business or government for a set period of time, in return for interest payments.

certificate of deposit (CD): A savings certificate issued by a bank when an investor deposits cash for a fixed period of time at a fixed interest rate. If the investor withdraws the money before the maturity date, there is often a penalty.

conservative investor: An investor who assumes no risk or minimal risk and has his or her money in cash and bonds.

credit risk: The risk that an investor will lose his or her principal or not receive interest payments should a borrower fail to repay a loan.

currency risk: The risk that changes in currency exchange rates may affect the returns of foreign investments. For example, if you own stocks in a Mexican company, their value is affected not only by changes in the price of those stocks but also by changes in the value of the peso compared to the U.S. dollar.

diversification: The spreading of an investor's money among different investments within one asset class. While diversification does not eliminate risk, it does help avoid unsystematic risk, which is the risk that comes when an investor's eggs are all in one basket.

dividend: A portion of a company's profits paid to an investor who owns stocks in the company.

duration: See *time*.

equity: A term used to describe a stock, also known as a share, which represents an investor's part ownership of a company. It is one of the main asset classes on the investment pyramid.

FDIC-insured: A term used to describe an investment that is insured by the Federal Deposit Insurance Corporation (FDIC). The standard insurance amount is $250,000 per depositor, per insured bank, for each account type.

fixed-income: A term used to describe investments, such as bonds, for which an investor receives fixed periodic interest payments and has the principal returned after a set period of time. Fixed-income is one of the main asset classes on the investment pyramid.

inflation: A rise in the general level of prices of goods and services over time. A good example of the effect of inflation is the rise in the cost of a gallon of milk over the past 10 years.

interest-rate risk: The risk that an investment's value will change due to a change in interest rates. For instance, when interest rates go up, bond prices go down; and when interest rates go down, bond prices go up.

international equities: Stocks in overseas companies.

"I Quit!" Account: The account that you pay a portion of your income into each month for retirement. This is the place where you put your long-term money.

large capitalization/large cap: Term used to describe stocks in a big company. For a company to be classified as large cap, its total stocks must have a high market value.

Life Happens Account: An account into which you pay a portion of your monthly income until it can cover 12 months of living expenses should you lose your source of income. It should not be drawn on for day-to-day expenses, only to cover emergencies.

liquidity risk: The risk that arises when an investment or asset cannot be sold quickly, so if prices fall quickly, the investor might not be able to prevent a loss.

market capitalization/market cap: A measure, used by investment professionals, of the size of a company. It is arrived at by multiplying the number of shares that are currently held by investors by the current market price of one share. The larger the number, the larger the company.

market timing risk: The risk in attempting to predict the direction of a market and invest accordingly. There is a risk that an investor will be out of the market at the best time or get back in at the worst time.

money-market account: A type of savings account that usually pays higher interest than a regular checking account. It normally requires a higher minimum balance, and there may be restrictions on the amount of withdrawals an investor can make.

plan: A series of steps that lead to a long-term financial goal.

political/economic risk: The risk that arises because the value of investments in a foreign country might be affected by political and economic changes within that country.

principal: In the investment world, a term for the amount of money originally invested, not including earnings, or the face value of a bond. (When used in relation to debt, the term means the amount borrowed or still owed on a loan, not including interest.)

principle: Core belief that serves as the foundation for what you do with your money.

priority: An action or task that you rank as more important and urgent than other actions and tasks.

quality: In relation to bonds, a measure of the dependability of the company you are loaning your money to and the probability of getting your money back.

reinvestment risk: The risk, most often associated with bonds, that future proceeds might have to be invested at a lower rate.

Rule of 72: A way of calculating how many years it will take to double a sum of money at a certain interest rate. You do this by dividing 72 by the interest rate.

share: See *equity*.

small capitalization/small cap: A term used to describe a stock with a relatively small market value. Investment professionals consider companies that are valued between $300 million and $2 billion to fall into this category.

something: What you need to save in order to have something. If you save nothing, you will always have nothing. Something will always be more than nothing.

spending plan/budget: A tool you use to tell your money where to go, instead of wondering where it went.

stock: See *equity*.

time: In relation to bonds, how long you are going to let someone borrow your money; also referred to in the finance industry as *duration*.

uncommon sense: The type of thinking you have to use so you do not make the same financial mistakes as everybody else.

unsystematic risk: Risk that affects an individual stock or a specific group of stocks, rather than a whole market.

U.S. Treasury bills: A type of bond backed by the U.S. government that matures in a set period of time, up to 12 months.

volatility: The degree of uncertainty about the size of rises and falls in an investment's value. The higher the volatility, the more dramatically the investment's value can rise or fall in any given period of time.

Acknowledgments

I would like to thank Derrell Crimm, who has been such a great friend and mentor. You were there for me during the good times and the bad. I have learned so much from you—not only the fundamental and technical aspects of the business—because you are also a great role model to follow in everyday life. I want to thank John Sileo for writing the foreword. It is such an honor to be able to call you my friend! I want to thank Darrell Moore for his expertise and guidance in the compliance arena, as without his help I wouldn't have been able to get this book out. Last but not least, I want to thank my editor, Vanessa Mickan, who was able to take my ideas and stories and package them together in a way that my readers will be able to get so much more out of this book.

WORKSHEETS

Spending Tracker

Item	1	2	3	4	5	6	7

Please visit www.repakfs.com to download an Adobe version of the worksheets.

8	9	10	11	12	13	14	15

Spending Tracker continued...

Item	16	17	18	19	20	21	22	23

Please visit www.repakfs.com to download an Adobe version of the worksheets.

24	25	26	27	28	29	30	31

SPENDING SUMMARY

Spending Category	Current Spending	
Giving		
Church		
Charity		
Total Giving		%
Saving		
Life Happens Account		
"I Quit" Account		
Total Saving		%
Housing		
Mortgage/Rent		
Second Mortgage		
Homeowner's/Renter's Insurance		
Electricity		
Gas/Heating Oil		
Water and Sewer		
Garbage		
Home Telephone (Landline)		
Cell Phone		
Personal Digital Device (PDA)		
Cable/Satellite Television		

Please visit www.repakfs.com to download an Adobe version of the worksheets.

Spending Category	Current Spending	
Internet Fees		
House Repair/Yard Work		
Storage		
Total Housing		%
Food		
Groceries		
Breakfasts Out		
Lunches Out		
Dinners Out		
Quick Stops (Coffee, Snacks)		
Vending Machines		
Total Food		%
Transportation		
Car Loan Payments		
Fuel and Oil		
Car Insurance		
Car Repairs		
Car Washes		
Bus/Train Fares		
License/Registration/Tax		
Tolls/Parking		
Total Transportation		%

Spending Summary continued...

Spending Category	Current Spending	
Clothing		
Self		
Spouse		
Children		
Laundry		
Dry Cleaning		
Alterations		
Total Clothing		%
Debt Payments		
Credit Card Payments		
Personal Loan Payments		
Student Loan Payments		
Total Debt Payments		%
Personal		
Health Insurance (if not deducted from your take-home pay)		
Medical Bills		
Dental Insurance and Bills		
Optometrist		
Medicines		
Vitamins, Supplements, Herbal Medicines		
Life Insurance		
Child Support		
Alimony		

Please visit www.repakfs.com to download an Adobe version of the worksheets.

Spending Category	Current Spending	
Hair and Beauty		
Music (CDs and downloads)		
Movies and DVD Rental and Purchase		
Video Games		
Alcoholic Beverages		
Tobacco Products		
Gifts (Birthday, Graduation, etc.)		
Education (Books, Tuition)		
Pets		
Hobbies		
Total Personal Spending		%
Grand Total		%

Note: To calculate the percentage for a category, take your monthly expense for the category, divide it by your monthly take-home pay, and multiply that by 100. For example, if your total monthly food expense was $450 and your monthly take-home pay was $3,000, you would do this calculation: ($450 ÷ $3,000) x 100 = 15%

SPENDING PLAN

Spending Category	Current Spending	Goal	
Giving			
Church			
Charity			
Total Giving			10
Saving			
Life Happens Account			
"I Quit" Account			
Total Saving			10
Housing			
Mortgage/Rent			
Second Mortgage			
Homeowner's/Renter's Insurance			
Electricity			
Gas/Heating Oil			
Water and Sewer			
Garbage			
Home Telephone (Landline)			
Cell Phone			
Personal Digital Device (PDA)			
Cable/Satellite Television			

Please visit www.repakfs.com to download an Adobe version of the worksheets.

160

Spending Category	Current Spending	Goal	
Internet Fees			
House Repair/Yard Work			
Storage			
Total Housing			30–40%
Food			
Groceries			
Breakfasts Out			
Lunches Out			
Dinners Out			
Quick Stops (Coffee, Snacks)			
Vending Machines			
Total Food			10–15%
Transportation			
Car Loan Payments			
Fuel and Oil			
Car Insurance			
Car Repairs			
Car Washes			
Bus/Train Fares			
License/Registration/Tax			
Tolls/Parking			
Total Transportation			15–20%

Spending Plan continued...

Spending Category	Current Spending	Goal	
Clothing			
Self			
Spouse			
Children			
Laundry			
Dry Cleaning			
Alterations			
Total Clothing			5–10%
Debt Payments			
Credit Card Payments			
Personal Loan Payments			
Student Loan Payments			
Total Debt Payments			5–10%
Personal			
Health Insurance (if not deducted from your take-home pay)			
Medical Bills			
Dental Insurance and Bills			
Optometrist			
Medicines			
Vitamins, Supplements, Herbal Medicines			
Life Insurance			
Child Support			
Alimony			

Please visit www.repakfs.com to download an Adobe version of the worksheets.

Spending Category	Current Spending	Goal	
Hair and Beauty			
Music (CDs and downloads)			
Movies and DVD Rental and Purchase			
Video Games			
Alcoholic Beverages			
Tobacco Products			
Gifts (Birthday, Graduation, etc.)			
Education (Books, Tuition)			
Pets			
Hobbies			
otal Personal Spending		10–15%	
rand Total		100%	

ote: To calculate the percentage for a category, take your monthly expense for the category, divide it by ur monthly take-home pay, and multiply that by 100. For example, if your total monthly food expense as $450 and your monthly take-home pay was $3,000, you would do this calculation: ($450 ÷ 3,000) x 100 = 15%

163

DEBT ASSESSOR

Debt	Interest Rate	Outstanding Balance	Minimum Payment	Actual Payment

Note: Once you have all of the information filled out, you will be able to put together a plan to get out of debt once and for all. I recommend that you go to powerpay.org to draw up your own get-out-of-debt plan.

Please visit www.repakfs.com to download an Adobe version of the worksheets.

About the Author

Steve Repak, CFP®, is an Army veteran, motivational speaker, consultant, and principal at Repak Financial Services. Steve has helped countless ordinary people turn their finances around with his inspiring personal finance presentations and one-on-one financial counseling.

As a former soldier, Steve went through basic training and knows what it means to give up old ways of thinking and retrain yourself to think differently. He has been in the same financial predicament that his audiences find themselves in—broke and in debt. More importantly, using the same tools he gives readers in *Dollars & Uncommon Sense,* he got himself out of that predicament.

When Steve was growing up, his family had little or no money. After graduating high school, he enlisted in the Army. There, he was just like most people, spending everything he made, living paycheck to paycheck, and not saving. When he left the Army after 12 years of service, he had racked up more than $32,000 in credit card debt.

Through his contacts he had made in the military, he was offered a job in finance. By observing what his wealthy clients did differently from the ones who were struggling, he discovered that it isn't how much you make but how you think about money that determines wealth.

Steve began to change the way he thought about money, and formulated his own plan to get out of debt and build his wealth.

Steve Repak was the 1995 Fort Bliss, Texas, Noncommissioned Officer of the Year and graduated Summa Cum Laude with a Bachelor of Science in Management Communications from Amridge University. He now works for himself as a highly successful Certified Financial Planner™ in Charlotte, North Carolina, where his lives with his wife and three children.